Women of Manipur

Women of Manipur

An Alternative Perspective

Salam Irene

ANSHAH Anshah Publishing House

Rs. 700; US$ 35

ISBN: 978-81-8364-103-6

First Published in India in 2014

Women of Manipur: An Alternative Perspective

Published by:
ANSHAH PUBLISHING HOUSE
LG, Pankaj Central Market, I.P. Ext.,
Patparganj, Delhi-110092, Tel: 22235152, 9810522367
Br.Off. 4617/18, Ansari Road, Darya Ganj,
New Delhi-110002, Tel: 9650028065

for
Mahen, Brandon, Crystal,
Varshaa, Darryn

Preface

This book retrieves women's position in history, because even today, gender studies find no place in the curriculum of most disciplines both at the graduate and post-graduate levels. The book is written from a gender perspective and largely confined to the urban centres of Manipur, especially Imphal. The focus of the book is on the contradictions inherent in the popular belief that women in Manipur enjoy a high status. Despite being accorded respect and honor at home, and extolled on the public platform, women are increasingly becoming recipients of a spiraling violence, to which there is no limit, both in the public domain and the private arena of the family. Much of the violence in the former, stems from the fact, that Manipur has been a conflict ridden state for decades, and the accompanying environment of uncertainty, fear and insecurity, act as triggers to up the quotient of violence. In the private domain of the family, the state is reluctant to intervene, despite the knowledge that domestic violence is a daily occurrence. In such a situation, the supposedly, empowered women become docile and subservient, even when their rights are trampled upon, as for instance, when a husband indulges in an extra-marital affair, the woman passively condones it, from fear of even more adverse repercussion, such as a second wife taking charge of the home. Some indigenous saying purport to portray that women in Manipur lead an easy, comfortable life, as their duties and responsibilities are 'only' confined to household affairs and management. The reality is that these supposedly easy tasks extract a heavy toll on women, who have to work all hours, who have to multi-task, and also supplement the family kitty by working outside the home. There is certainly no equitable distribution of household chores and corresponding responsibilities. Most women in Manipur are working, but as most also work in the unorganized sector, at the level of subsistence, they are deprived of rights enjoyed by salaried women in the organized sector such as earned leave, maternity and health benefits etc.

There are several examples of women who have succeeded in cracking the glass ceiling despite all odds. But these are a small minority—the majority of women are not empowered in the true sense of the term.

Contents

1

Introduction

It is a truism that in all present day discourses centering around women, Violence Against Women (VAW) occupies a prominent place. Despite ongoing efforts to improve the status of women as also to provide safety nests both in public and private spaces VAW continues to escalate. So we need to question the reasons for women's vulnerability to violence, and why strategies put in place for women's empowerment are not working. VAW is not confined merely to Manipur or India, it is a worldwide all-pervasive phenomena. Just as VAW has a close connection with women's status and position, it also has an intimate connection with the ideology of Patriarchy, especially in the context of Manipur.

Manipur, the Land of Jewels—Sanaleibak, is a state in North East India with a population of 2.7 million, sharing a common international border with Myanmar. With the changes that have occurred in geopolitics, and because of the 'Look East Policy' of the Government of India, the Strategic importance of Manipur has grown exponentially, as it is for India, the 'Gateway to South East Asia'. Moreover, the people of Manipur have their own distinct identity, culture, ethos, way of life and self-governing system. The state, originally a monarchical kingdom boasts of a recorded history dating from 33 A.D. It preserved its independent existence for a long period of time, it only came under colonial rule when Manipur was defeated in the Anglo Manipur War of 1891. It became independent in 1947. But was merged into the Indian Union in 1949, but only became a state as late as 1972.

The population of Manipur originally comprised of the 'Meiteis' who dwell in the Imphal Valley, and the tribals—Nagas and Kukis who dwelt largely in the hills which comprise 9/10th of the state. In the seventeenth century Muslims (Pangals) made their entry into Manipur followed by Brahmins in the 18th century when the Meiteis converted to Hinduism. They were followed by people from other parts of India, especially in the 20th century. Manipur represents a mosaic of plural cultures and people. If the current ethnicity of Manipur valley population could be broad-banded by the two majority groups viz. the Muslims and Meiteis (composite of the Hindu and Sanamahis), then that of the Manipur hills could likewise be overreached by another two: the Nagas and the Kukis. The only two discernible differences being first, that the valley society long since evolved a pluralistic society, and apparently passed through a detribalization process onto modernization, and second, that two-thirds of the state humans congregate in the valley measuring 700 sq. miles or 2,238 kms. while the balance one-third spread out over the remaining 8000 sq. miles or 20,089 kms. hill areas of the state[1].

As to the common ancestry of the three autochthon groups viz. the Meities, Nagas and Kukis (Muslims came in King Khagemba's reign 1597-1652 A.D.), the British ethnologist T.C. Hodson wrote: "Tradition affords link which makes the Nagas, the Kukis and the Manipuris descent from a common ancestor, who had three sons who became the progenitor of those tribes, the tradition, which is widely spread, agrees in its many versions in assigning the primacy of the descent to the Kukis, the next place being given to the Nagas, while the Manipuris are said to be children of the youngest of the three brothers[2].

Various ethnic groups belonging to the Southern Mongoloid group; the Tibeto—Burmans, the Indo—Aryans and a sizeable section of the Tais (Shans) came to Manipur from pre-historic times down to the present day. The present ethnic groups of Manipur viz. the Meities, the Naga tribes, the Kuki Chin tribes and other Indian communities are the descendants of those migrating people[3]. In pre-colonial Manipur, under a feudal dynastic system of authority relations, ethnic categories subsisted with frequent interactions which could be economic interdependence, barter of essential goods and supplies, participation in community rituals and of course, fierce protection of collectivities, village and clan settlements from external threat. Mutual trust was founded on the system of reciprocity[4].

In a recent survey conducted by the National Crime Bureau, Assam was rated as the state in North East India leading in VAW. However, this does not mean that the people of Manipur can be lulled into complacency—the crimes recorded for Manipur[5] are merely the tip of the iceberg, as most women who suffer violence, especially rape or other forms of sexual assault, prefer to remain silent for fear of repercussion in the form of social ostracism, or from shame, and a plethora of complex emotions and feelings. The common perception in Manipur is that women enjoy a very high status especially in comparison to women in other parts of India. To some extent, the perception is correct, but it is also riddled with contradictions and complexities, which make it difficult to accept such a statement at face value. One of the early writers on 'Feminism' in Manipur stated that Meitei women make crucial economic contributions and hold a distinctive position in social, religious and political life. Within an overall patrilineal framework, women are thus able to develop a power base and a group solidarity, strengthened by various women's organizations. Women's collective power in the political arena, hitherto a male domain, was made evident during the 'women's wars' (Nupi Lan) in 1904 and 1939 against colonial policies[6]. Fast forward to the present day: despite the absence of a dowry system till very recently, a salaried, professional male, who espouses the cause of women's empowerment vociferously on every occasion on a public platform, in the private realm of the family, demands not just a conventional dowry, but a good size piece of land in his own name: there is no protest from the bride, her women relatives and even women's groups, they weakly accede to this irrational demand. This incident occurs in the Meitei community. In a tribal community, an exclusive church-based woman's organization outlines strategies to improve the quality of life of its constituent members, both in the spiritual and temporal realm. But before the strategies could be implemented, the male members of the church reprimanded the women for arriving at decisions without consulting them. Ultimately no improvement can be effected. A modern educated woman with a high social standing introduces herself to an older woman at a social gathering in the words: 'I am the wife of Mr. A': she subsumes her individual identity. Among the uneducated, the husband of a Nepali hard working woman is hospitalized. The man demands her presence at the hospital 24 hours a day, even when his condition is not critical, he will not permit her to even go home and take a bath. Fear of the 'patti parmeswar' keeps, her obediently at his side. It is pertinent to reflect on the saying of the Talmund: "If I am not for myself, who will be for me"[7]. Are women then a marginalized section of society? What has been written about tribal women in Manipur is quite relevant to Meitei women as well. 'Tribal women are more exploited and marginalized, they do not have representation or voice in village or clan councils. While the subjugation is rooted in patriarchy it is sanctified by custom and reinforced by the state[8]. The Social Welfare Minister A.K. Mirabai on International Women's Day 2013, lamented that women's participation in administration remains nominal, even though 33 per cent seats have been reserved for women in Panchayats and Municipal Councils. The women representatives function just as namesakes, while the actual work or decision making is done by their husbands. If women continue to depend on men, neither the Indian Constitution nor any laws would succeed in alleviating their socio-economic and political position. The basic reason for the inferiority complex attached to women is their dependence on men[9].

In fact, by giving women the centrality of the family, they are made to believe that they are respected, and given the most coveted position. In fact they are intelligently being kept away from administration and politics, which are the domains of power. However high, the women's status in any given society, as long as there is no equality and freedom in the realm of politics, economy and decision—making, the patriarchal element will reign strong and supreme[10]. Care and nurturing of family members and the responsibility for household chores does not devolve on women alone, by any statute of law. Tasks usually assigned to women within the home such as cooking or washing of clothes, in the public domain is usually performed by 'elite' male chefs and the common washerman (dhobi). Yet in most households in Manipur there is no egalitarian distribution of household chores and responsibilities. Rather women fall prey to the 'compassion trap', i.e. they are made to feel that they exist to serve others, to provide tenderness and compassion. The totally compassionate woman contributes to society's well being, by freeing men of all domestic responsibility, so that men can tend to the more important concerns of work business, science, politics, etc. Even working women are not exempt, they tend to opt more for professions like social work, teaching, nursing, etc. Even the lone woman Cabinet Minister in Manipur has been given the portfolio of Social Welfare—an illustration of sterio-typing the role and work of women. As Rekha Roy puts it: Women bear the triple burden of job, housework and children, because, first of all, they are willing to bear this mantle of three fold responsibility due to social conditioning, and second, because it is in the interest of men that this type of social order continue as it advantages them[11].

Patriarchy permeates all aspects of women's lives—it is an ideology that assigns cardinal importance to the 'pater' or father, who as head of the family exercises absolute jurisdiction/ power over all its constituent members. Patriarchy impacts all women in varying degrees, rich, poor, educated, illiterate, urban and rural, empowered and disempowered. A society is considered patriarchal when men, establish or inherit a social order where they dominate positions of power or authority or when important achievements and historical events are attributed to the actions of men[12]. In Manipur the success of the Nupilans is solely attributed to women, but despite this recognition of their role in historical events as also of their contribution to the well being of society in their role as 'Meira Paibis' (torch bearers) and as 'Nisha Bandhs' they still continue to be dominated by men in their homes. For instance a Nisha Bandh (a women who actively works to eradicate alcohol abuse on the streets) will submit to a beating from a drunken husband at home, to maintain peace within the family. So the family home which should function as a haven of comfort and safety, instead often resounds with cries of women who are subjected to violence within their own homes. It is important to take cognizance of the fact that 'gender equality is not just about property and who inherits it. It is about who does what and who has access and control over what resources'[13]. For instance in a state with an agrarian economy there are many women cultivators who contribute equally with male cultivators to food production and sustainability of natural resources like community ponds, forest land etc. But decisions regarding agrarian matters are made by men; moreover as women cultivators have the sole responsibility of the family, even if they desire, they do not have time to meet with agricultural experts whether from the government or from non-government organizations, because of their work-load, and so consciously or unconsciously allow men to make all important decisions regarding cultivation. It is the men who usually attend agricultural trainings and benefit from workshops and decide what new seeds or technologies are to be introduced in the agrarian sector, especially when such trainings/workshops are held outside the state, or at a considerable distance from the women cultivator's homes.

The concept of empowerment is often confused with freedom of mobility—for instance Manipuri women are extremely mobile, but this does not mean that they are empowered. 'Empowerment means being able to have access to information and an informed choice'. This is especially relevant with regard to family planning. Women must have the option 'of spacing children' and exercising 'freedom to choose the size of the family'[14]. However this freedom is generally not a reality. 'Even among the most educated families where men are expected to be more gender conscious, the woman spends much of her time in the kitchen[15]. Educated men justify this action with the logic that if they assumed the tasks of cooking at home, it would lead to constant feuds in the family because such men would then continuously criticize meals prepared by women since they were now well conversant with how to cook delicious culinary delights.

By idealizing wifehood and motherhood and projecting women as the epitome of tolerance and suffering, the patriarchal societies carry out the domestication of the female without much problem. The society is able to maintain its equilibrium as no woman dares to claim an equal status with the dominant sex. Society establishes the virtue of 'ideal womanhood' as being able to say 'yes' to everything that is dictated to her, and being non re-active to what is being done to her. As a result, a woman is taught to tell herself and others that she is happy, even when she faces harassment and humiliation for being a woman. In spite of the fact, that there is a lot of inner resistance and emotions against such a social system from the female side, very often they put on a mask and pretend to be happy and balanced, because they have learned that open resistance can only invite gossip, criticism and social isolation[16]. Although this statement has been made in the context of Khasi society which is matrilineal, it is equally applicable to Manipur. For instance, a young independent salaried woman professional meekly carries out the task assigned to her by her older husband—the task of putting on his shoes and tying the laces, after of course cleaning and polishing them—she also has to remove her husband's shoes when he retires to bed, or when he is desirous of changing his shoes for more comfortable footwear. Sometimes, young widows are forced to marry the brother of their deceased husband, especially in tribal communities—the women's acquiescence is taken for granted. As Lois Tyoon remarks: 'A patriarchal woman is a woman that has internalized the norms and values of patriarchy'[17].

References

1. Salam Irene, Manipur: Land, People, Demography, p. 58, cit., T.S. Gangte: Kuki Naga Ethnicity in Current Manipur Polity, cit. in Madhu

Rajput, Editor, *Understanding North East India: Cultural Diversities, Insurgency and Identities.*

2. Salam Irene, *op. cit.*, p. 59.
3. *Ibid.*, p. 60, *op. cit.*, Gangmumei Kabui, *History of Manipur*, Vol. 1, Pre-Colonial Period, pp. 15-23.
4. *Ibid.*, p. 61, *op. cit.* Lokendra Arambam (2005): *Ethnicity and Politics of Identity: The Manipur Experience.*
5. Manjusri Chaki-Sircar, Feminism in a *Traditonal Society, Women of the Manipur Valley*, 1984, Preface, pp. viii-ix.
6. Rekha Roy, *Women's Rights in India: A Feminist Pespective*, p. 188.
7. 304, Crimes against Women, 63 cases of rape cit. in the *Sangai Express*, 18th June 2013.
8. Priyadarshini M. Gangte, *Gender Bias in Manipuri Society* cit., Tiplut Nongbri.
9. *The Sangai Express*, 8th March 2013.
10. Celine Augustine, *Matriliny in Transition*, p. 200.
11. Rekha Roy, *op. cit.*, pp. 179, 184.
12. *Ibid.*, p. 78, at. Barbara R. Cruikshank, 'Patriarchy'.
13. Patricia Mukhim, Myths, Tradition and Identity, Women in Matriliny, p. 217, cit in. Celine Augustine, *op. cit.*
14. *Ibid.*, *op. cit.*, p. 221.
15. *Ibid.*, *op. cit.*, p. 217.
16. Celine Augustine *op. cit.*, pp. 9-10.
17. Lois Tyson, *Critical Theory Today*, 2nd Edition, Routledge 2006, New York.

2

Women's Status

Internal Contradictions, Role of Women

British ethnographers have in their descriptions of Manipur women's status and role, clearly delineated the dichotomy that exists in the high status generally ascribed to women. E.W. Dun writing in 1886, remarked: 'The women in Manipur, married or unmarried are not confined in zenanas, as they are in Bengal or Hindustan, neither do they cover their faces before strangers. They are very industrious. Most of the work of the country, except the heaviest is performed by them—they are the mainstay of the family circle. All the marketing is done by women, all the work of buying and selling in public and the carrying to an fro of the articles to be sold, whilst at home, they are busily employed in weaving and spinning. It would be difficult to find a more industrious woman in India than the Manipuri. With all their industry and usefulness, women hold a very inferior social position[1]. This description is both an ode to women, and at the same time clearly indicates that despite being so industrious, the social worth of woman is not compatible with her accomplishments. T.C. Hodson largely concurs with Dun's estimate. The women hold a high and free position in Manipur, all the internal trade and exchange of the produce of the country being managed by them[2]. This tribute also clearly recognizes women's contribution to the economy of Manipur, but as this contribution is not accounted for in the GDP of the state, women's economic contribution is greatly undervalued and this adversely impacts their status. Yet in the land which has given the Meira Paibi movement to the world, as also the Nupi-Lan, where women are placed on a high pedestal in the public domain, they continue to be at the receiving end within the walls of their homes, as well as face discrimination in every other aspect of life. Rapes, murder, molestation, abduction of women are the extreme forms of VAW. People have publicly demonstrated their stand against these acts which have become some sort of a trend. However, there are the subtle, not publicly acknowledged practices that go unreported most of the time. Wife beating is more or less an accepted practice, mostly enacted within the confines of one's home. Eve teasing is passed off as one of the phases in the development of a young boy. The character of girls or women being questioned at the time her modesty is outraged is one of the ugliest manifestations of today's society in Manipur. Crimes against women in Manipur have mostly centered around the social hypocrisy that has become institutionalized, and an accepted way of life. As long as this mindset persists, women will continue to be second class citizens[3].

But the early literature narrates the achievements of many outstanding women in the annals of Manipur's history. And, the high status ascribed to Manipuri Women may be viewed in the early period, by analyzing the role of 'Yabirok' in making her son Nongda Lairen Pakhangba, a king of Kangla[4]. Laisna, Queen of Nongda Lairen Pakhangba (33-154 A. D.) was actively associated with the social and cultural life of the Kangla people[5]. The pre-colonial state was a gender sensitized state. Active participation in economic/social management was encouraged[6]. In fact one, school of thought postulates that when Queen Lainaotabi reigned, a matriarchal system was prevalent in Manipur. In support of this view, it has been cited, that when Laisana (Laisana) got married to Nongda Lairen Pakhangba, she was Head of the 'Kucha' and along with nine women Phamdou (Ministers) looked after administrative affairs, but Meidingu Pakhangba constituted a 'Kuchu' with nine male Phamdou, and introduced patriarchy[7]. In contrast we have Nungshongshu who withheld the funeral ceremony of her husband

and Queen Linthoingambi (1432-1467 A.D.) who quelled a Tangkhul rebellion in the absence of her husband[8].

Meitei tradition does not permit a woman to ascend the throne, but she may act as a Dowager Queen in the case of a minor ascending the throne[9]. In the royal palace the old women wielded great authority—there was even a court by old women consisting of nine members. The members consisted of the former Queens, the King's aunt and his Mapi (wet nurse)[10]. The court looked after the code of conduct of the royal members—they even had the authority to punish the king, and many a Queen and consorts were punished by them—Charairongba was beaten on his back with a burning torch, and made to pay five lao pari (rice fields) to the three women who carried out the action known as Nongthil Chaibi Lou[11].

In Meitei scripture, a power struggle between the Almighty and His consort, the Supreme Mother is depicted. Although the mother along with her elder son is enshrined in every family in the south-west corner of a house, the female principle is subsumed into the male principle. The 'Emoinu' myth prescribes the role of women: housekeeping and motherhood. This lends credence to patriarchy[12].

The position and status of women in any given society is reflected in the legendary and mythological figures of women. Khamnu, Thoibi and Thambalnu fall in the first category, whereas Leimarel Shidabi, Iraileima, Yumjao Leima fall in the second category. Prior to the establishement of colonial rule (1891) outstanding women were many, such as Chingkhei Tanbi, Linthoingambi, Tangjakhombi, Gomti, Kumudini, to name a few. Both Linthoingambi and Tangjakhombi used clever ruses to defeat their enemies[13].

It is believed that since the time of Pakhangba, 'Pacha Loishang' was established as a Court of Women presided over by the Queen[14]. Women of the Pacha bore titles such as Thumja-Qrungbi (Mistress of Salt Trade), Ngarunbi (Mistress of Fish Collection), Phisarungbi (Mistress of Cloth Manufacture), Loikhomsang Hanjabi (Mistress of Tribute Collection House).

These women's functions were separately organized, there was no dispute in power and jurisdiction with similar posts held by men. There were no instances of their seeking official space, emoluments, privileges, status differentiation, from the official class—posts were more functional and associative, rather than ceremonial[15]. Pantoibi, the Mangang princess is given the status of a multi-faceted goddess by the Meiteis; she is often described as 'Thanglon Haikup Chenbi'[16]. Even today during the Lai Haraoba, the Maibis perform the sword dance, showering reverence to the Goddess[17]. After the advent of Hinduism in the eighteenth century, there were some changes in the status of women. Although free movement by women in Hindu culture is restricted, in Manipur only to some degree were upper class women affected, the common women continued to enjoy mobility required for the performance of economic functions. A positive impact was the inclusion of the Chief Queen in the reign of Garib Niwaz. Moreover, even after marriage, the palace maintained contact with royal daughters, many of whom occupied important posts in the palace Loishangs[18].

In describing the Meira Paibees, Lokendra Arambam has traced the sources of women's strength to the traditional roots of their philosophy, and to the intrinsic character of their civilization. He writes: 'Meira Paibee became a particular phenomenon in women's pro-active interventions in times of social stress and crises since the 1980's. They work in the culture of traditional practices and behaviour: their sense of justice and equity are derived from natural human laws. Pre-Hindu Meitei thought, beliefs and culture set the standards of their behaviour and action. Both male and female principles are equally contributory to en-gendering of the cosmic cycle and sensuous balance of the female (pee) and male (paa) polarities. Collective participation in rituals and ceremonies also had a gender sensitizing accent, to enhance the physical health, morals and reproductive capacity of Manipuri women[19]. In fact, women of all ages and conditions participated actively, in socio-religious festivals like Yaoshang, Hiyangtanaba, Laiharouba, sports and games. Women priestesses—'maibis' were important in the performance of religious rites, rituals, dances, divination, singing, prophesy[20]. But when Meidingu Khagemba (1597-1652 A.D.) established 'Yoiren Loishang' (Academy of Preists), he placed the Maibis under their control. And in the reign of Meidingu Pamheiba (1709-1748 A.D.), the indigenous Meitei religion of the Maibi and Maiba gave way to Vaishnavite Hinduism. However women still continued to be held in high status—during the reign of Meidingu Chandrakirti, the Queen Mother was greatly honoured, but after her death, the 'Lakkhong' (Women's Kuchu) ceased to exist. But female power remained entrenched in practices of the Maibis (they lead the annual Lai Harouba procession—pre Vaishnative practice) and are held in high esteem[21]. The Maibis were the original Wakma of the land[22].

Since society and polity in Manipur was organized through the concept of blood relationship and kin, women were closely associated with the source of power in the centre. Ambitious and patriotic citizens seeking court favours, married their daughters and sisters into royalty, and powerful, capable nobles got their wives from amongst the ladies in court. Certain institutions of women in the traditional polity helped shape and mould the character of women in the early state: one, the cultural institution of women's affairs—The Pacha Loishang (Office of Women established during Paikhomba's reign 1666-1697) and the Sana-Keithel (Golden Market) which developed into a full fledged economic and social centre in the sixteenth century. The deliberations of the first were presided over by the Queen Mother assisted by other ladies. The subjects under their jurisdiction comprised many issues—domestic violence, wife-beating, adultery, disputed paternity, divorce, wrong indiscretions by the King in sexual relationships, etc. Fines could be imposed on royalty—punishment was harsh.

The Sana Keithel was established by King Khagemba in 1614 A.D., a centre of barter/exchange, a social centre for fashion, an indigenous media centre where news and events were discussed, and a space for royal and commoner interactions. The King often visited the market, and nearness to the source of power, helped the market women to keep abreast of political events. The act of discipline and punishment which the feudal kings meted out to offending citizens were displayed in the Keithel, codes of behaivour and ethics would be instilled into the public.

The market was the nerve centre in the state's economy, personal inter-communal integration was very much a factor. The women of the market by virtue of their cross-cultural interactions and deep involvement in social affairs were alert, extroverted, independent. Incidents of occasional Keithel Kaiba (disruption in attendance of the market) marked vital crises in the polity, women often refused to follow state commands, disagreed upon decisions which they felt was against their perceived sense of justice. Desertion of the market was a sign of political acts of defiance, voluntarily initiated by women[23].

But in the Meitei community, women enjoy no property rights. The burden is felt more in the case of widowed women, since they take over the responsibility of running the family. However they play a significant role in some religious rituals and practices. One of the best examples of their participation can be seen in the Lai Haraoba festival (Festival to please the Deities). Here, the 'maibi' plays an indispensable part in performing the rituals and giving offerings to the Gods. She directs all the rituals. Meitei women also play a significant role in the whole process of the festival, and also participate in other rituals of the community—procuring/ arranging articles required for the Puja, performing kirtans' at weddings and occasions like Janmasthami[24].

It is evident that both primary and secondary data support the premise of the high status of women, but in accepting this premise, the question arises as to why Manipuri women especially in recent decades have become extremely vulnerable to violence. Especially as in the context of Meitei women, who reside in the valley, custom makes special provision for widowed divorced and unmarried daughters, by giving them a right of residence in their parents' home. Women inherit their mother's property, and have rights on their own dowry, which is to be returned after a divorce. Stridhan (women's wealth) is composed of a women's inherited wealth, her dowry, and her own savings[25]. This is perhaps why Mrs. Grimwood remarked: 'Manipur is do not shut up their women, as in the custom in most parts of India, and they are more enlightened and intelligent in consequence[26]. The role, image and status of Meitei women has been described by Y. Buddhichandra in his book 'Imoinu Ahonggbige Tungnapham—as a socio-ethical code of conduct developed on the basis of various ancient Puyas. Role of women covers all spheres of life—domestic, socio-economic, cultural, political, religious. Widows and divorcees were allowed to remarry or lead a life of their own. For instance Angoupampa Kyamba, the king of Angom took king Lamkyamba's (1512-1523) widow, Queen Changning—Phabi, mother of Nongyinphaba as wife. But this does not mean that society treated them equally as other women, men who married them as also their offspring were banned from attending certain religious rites and rituals such as Lai-Haraoba, inheriting Pibapham[27].

In Meitei society women as life-givers are viewed from the perspective of reproduction, both women and men combined contribute to both biological and food production in harmony with the seasons of nature: man is the facilitator of the natural cycle, woman is privileged to be a part of the same[28]. The position of women in early societies of Manipur could be termed as high, as societies exhibited matrilineal as well as matriarchal characteristics. In recent times, some scholars are of the opinion that the early matriarchal societies in Manipur were led by Lady Shamans or Maibis[29]. In the Puya, 'Thirel Layat', Laikhurambi is depicted as a ruler of ten thousand lainuras[30]. Many Puyas, especially the clan genealogies known as 'Meihoubaron', recorded the clan progenitors as women, and many a time, only the name of the mother is given, for instance in the 'Sakok Lamlen', it is written that 'Kangba' born to Sinleima Leitung Ninthou Chanu, ruled the land[31].

In tribal society as in Meitei society, patriarchy dominates, yet women are accorded both respect and honour. This is illustrated in the special power accorded to Tangkhul Naga Women who are honoured with the title of 'Pukhareila' (facilitator) they intervene in feuds between clans and villages, and bring about an amicable solution. As a warrior's status was linked during the historical period with the number of heads of enemies that he killed and brought back to his home village, feuds were common, and the Pukhareila was kept extremely busy (Customary law prevents/forbids harm being inflicted on women). In the sphere of religion, Tangkhul women enjoyed the right to perform sacrifices at the end of the harvest (most Tangkhul festivals are associated with the different phases in the cycle of cultivation) to the Goddess of Wealth 'Phungjuphilua'. For this purpose, a special 'mother's seat (Ava Pamkhong) is installed and reserved for her[32]. In recent times this same tradition is enacted on the occasion of 'Mother's Day' in most Christian Churches—mothers are recognized for their great contribution to the welfare and continued harmonious existence of both family and society and are honoured with special prayers, blessings, gifts and a celebratory meal. The above mentioned custom is also prevalent among the Maram Nagas, indicating that Naga women command respect and honour in society. A Maram Khullen Queen viz. Pei Hinga took the revolutionary step of abolishing a discriminatory practice derogatory to women experiencing difficult labour. M-bong Katai (death in childbirth) sometimes occurred—the pregnant mother who could not give birth naturally, was removed from the house to a place away from it, and she was given no assistance in childbirth, very often both mother and child died. This is considered a bad omen, all the possessions of the deceased are removed: the villagers do not join in her funeral. Inter-marriage among different 'Khel' of Maram Khullen village were tabooed, the Queen permitted inter marriage in 1975. Also, as per tradition the King or Queen performs certain rituals before cultivation commences. Unless the King plants the first seed, the village is barred from cultivation. This was changed by the Queen in 1981, to permit the villagers to start cultivation in time. The Queen of Maram Pei-Hinga removed many restrictions imposed on women, and helped to eliminate some old, ugly, superstitions that hampered female progress[33].

Naga women suffer no discrimination on account of sex-in that widows can remarry. 'Being a classless society, Naga women enjoy rights and privileges guaranteed under Naga customary law'[34]. But Johnstone observed, that Naga girls/women age quickly as a result of 'hard toil' associated with cultivation and carrying of heavy loads in hilly terrain[35]. Moreover, in Naga society, women have no share in the landed property of her father or her husband, except that acquired by the husband after marriage. Haimendorf states that 'many women in more civilized parts of India may well envy the women of Naga Hills, their high status and their happy life: and if you measure the cultural level of people by the social position and personal freedom of its women, you will think twice before looking down on the Nagas as savages'[36].

Among the Zeliangrong Naga tribes women have complete authority over all domestic matters, be it sale or purchase of handicrafts, shawls and domestic animals, excluding cattle. But they are prohibited from taking an active part in social and public affairs. As far as right to inheritance is concerned, women have no right to family property, because when they marry, they become a member of their husband's family and clan. However, the Naga woman in the case of death of a husband, does not lose her right over the belongings of her husband. If she remarries, she has to renounce this right, except if she marries the brother or near relative of her deceased husband[37]. In comparison with other tribes, the Zeliangrong women enjoy more privileges and power—they can choose their groom and even initiate divorce. Besides their important role in running and maintenance of the house, they play a vital part in lineage affairs, but in religion, they are barred from participating in family rites such as 'Duikhangmei', Laokhangmei, etc. The high status of the women is illustrated by the activities of the national freedom fighter Haipei Rani Gaidinliu[38]. Her story and activities are 'found in many pages of the History of Independent India'[39].

Despite their privileges, many taboos are imposed on the women—non adherence results in misfortune. For example, women cannot step over men, they cannot become priestesses unlike the maibis in Meitei society, they are also barred from wearing male shawls—haora/luirim (There are separate shawls woven for women). Other restrictions prevent them from sitting cross legged, touching the arms of warriors, participating in hunts, loosening their hair before village elders, or sleeping with a husband, prior to the latter going to war or for a hunt, also entering the perimeter of a wrestling bout, or even commenting on it. They are not taken into confidence at times of war because of their 'loose tongues', which also give rise to quarrels within clans and with neighbours[40].

Just like Naga women, the status of Kuki women is equivocal in that Kuki women are entrusted with great responsibility in the domain of the family and home—they are given honour and respect but 'customary law is largely gender insensitive—women are deprived of inheritance of landed property. There is a persistence of patrilineal tradition: Kuki society is characterized by an unequal division of labour and responsibilities within the household, based on unequal power relations[41]. According to C.P. Haokip—the low status, of the Thadou Kuki women is due to the practice of 'bride-price'. Parents practically sell their daughters to be wives and they demand a certain price for them. The facts are that the girl cultivates her parents fields and performs the household duties, and if any man wants her to do the same for him, he must compensate the parents for the loss of an able bodied servant[42]. This statement contrasts with that of T.J. Khothang and H.K. Khenthang who assert that the system of bride price is never in the sense of, buying or selling of a human being, but rather, compensating the family for parting with a daughter[43]. Nevertheless the bride price is fixed in monetary terms calculated according to the worth of the women's labour although the 'man' (bride price) is not paid in cash but in the form of gongs, beads, mithuns, etc. Diamond is of the opinion that 'the most important institution in the history of marriage is that of bride price'[44]. Bride price in one sense, enhances woman's status in that 'an accomplished bride fetches a higher price—it has a social value. The bride price further is matched by a reciprocal dowry given by the girls' parents. The worth of the latter enhances the standing of the bride in society[45]. The 'unpaid portion' of the bride price (it is not all paid at the time of marriage) 'implies that his (groom's) wife and relatives are precious, as the precious stones and assets yet to be paid'[46].

Divorce whether initiated by the woman or man results in degradation of the status of woman. This is clearly manifest when the corpse of a 'Nungkih' (divorced woman) is to be disposed off. The dead woman's body which ordinarily would have been taken for burial outside through the front door is instead taken through a hole made in the wall. This discrimination is now extinct[47].

The position of Kuki women has been described in Kuki literature. K. Kipgen writes 'the duties of a Thadou housewife is much less in comparison with those of her husband, she is responsible only for household chores'. But these household chores according to a Kuki lady comprises of back-breaking labour from not merely dawn to dusk, but inclusive of many more additional hours. Khamkam describes Paite women: 'the mother was loved by all but not given a position in the home. She worked day and night like a servant, was rebuked, insulted, not praised and honoured for her services[48].

But, women do play a significant role in the traditional life of the Kukis. This is exemplified in the practice of 'Longman' (corpse price). This is the price of a woman when she dies—the price is claimed by her father, elder/younger sons, in the father's absence, as a token of love and affection between the uterine kinsmen. This practice or price has to be paid to her sons as well. The practice indicates the high status of the woman within the family. But if a woman does not give birth to a son or sons, it is considered a disgrace to her father and brothers, who cannot claim Longman'[49]. Kuki women also have the privilege of performing 'Chang-ai (a ceremony linked to the successful cultivation of paddy, the staple of Kuki diet).

On Meitei Pangal women (Muslims) not much has been written perhaps because the Pangals only came to Manipur in the seventeenth century. The first settlers, all prisoners of war were not accompanied by women, but the Manipuri King Khagemba gave them Meitei women to marry; as a result there was a fusion of Islamic traditions and practices with Meitei traditions and practices. The Meitei Pangals were a family community where all members contributed to the process of agricultural production especially women. However women were basically enjoined to conscientiously carry out all the duties associated with the family and homestead, and in the public realm, to abide by the injunctions of the Holy Quran. But marriage rituals except the contract entered into, were largely modeled on Meitei customs. Despite polygamy being permitted under Islamic law, the incidence was negligible in Manipur. (The population of Muslims in Manipur was only 37,197 in 1951 rising to 1,90,939 in 2001. According to Census 2011, it has now reached the figure of 1,95,533). Women, most of whom reside in rural areas are largely confined to the domestic domain, and prevented from intermingling freely with men. A Muslim woman who marries outside her community is ostracised, this does not apply to a Pangal man who marries a non-Muslim. Women's primary duty is to please her husband—hence her status is subsumed under that of her husband[50]. But in contrast, Meitei Pangal women did not cover themselves with a *burqah*—as most women are working women this would have impeded both their work as also mobility. But when a quest for identity began at the end of the nineteenth century, rules for women as also men became more strict in line with Quranic injunctions. A minute proportion of women adopted the *burqah* when they ventured out to the public domain. Although the women especially mothers are respected, they were denied education till very recently. The most striking feature of Manipuri Muslim women's economic role is their direct participation in extra-familial economic activities—care of livestock, marketing, selling of goods, etc. Women because of the nature of their work, and because of their close proximity to each other in the market place (in the Ima Keithels—Women's Markets) forge bonds which give birth to a collective solidarity. In the Nupilan of 1939 Muslim women also participated, as also in other movements of the late 1990's and of the first decade of the 21st century, as the 18th June uprising of 2001, and others. However Muslims women do not have freedom to choose their life partner, to plan their family, to divorce, to remarry[51]. In recent years, Meitei Pangals women have formed organizations to improve the quality of life, especially in their own community. But a practice derogatory to women exists: divorcees force their ex-wives to resume marriage, (which is forbidden) without having been married to another man. They hire a man to marry temporarily the ex-wife and divorce her after a few days i.e. Nikah Khutnek (hired wedlock)[52]. The concept of an ideal woman in Manipuri mythology applies to the Pangal women as they are descendants of Meitei women. "According to the deity Imoinu, an ideal woman is one who is faithful to her husband, who regards her husband as divine and worships him, who obey orders and is submissive to the husband, who eats only when her husband has eaten. The shaping of such an ideal woman begins from childhood, with the active collaboration of the mothers. The daughter is brought up in such a way that she always feels inferior to her brothers[53]. Muslim women in Manipur are at a great disadvantage compared to their counterparts in other communities. Rigid patriarchy, social customs and traditions, like restriction on movement, early marriage and misuse of personal laws particularly on talaq, adoption and guardianship of children, maintenance and inheritance, have hindered the social empowerment of women[54]. Even though theoretically a divorced wife is entitled to provisions and maintenance, in reality, divorced women hardly get these benefits. They fail to get back the 'Mehr' (bride-price) promised in the Nikah-Nama[55].

There is a sizeable section of non-Manipuri women, primarily residing in the capital city of Imphal. Most of the women are wives, daughters, sisters of non-Manipuri businessmen who have settled in the state. During the period of colonial rule these businessmen were favoured by the British especially the Marwaris, who were able to dominate and appropriate for themselves much of the trade of Manipur. The wives of these businessmen however enjoy restricted mobility, because of age old traditions which confined a woman to the home, and in recent decades because of the absence of law and order, which confines women in a cocoon of insecurity. However, the women participate in all social and religious functions, beautifully attired and adorned with jewellery. However as most of these women live in the two main bazaars of Imphal they do not possess much visibility, and nothing much is known of their contribution to society.

However, they are a number of professional women working in different disciplines like health care, (doctors and nurses, pathologists etc.) academia, (schools, colleges, universities) as entrepreneurs, (especially in the beauty-related business), as fitness instructors, in the administrative and judicial service, as missionaries. These women usually enjoy a high status because of their contribution in various disciplines and because of their financial independence. However, women have to multi-task work both at home and outside. Nevertheless they do enjoy a privileged position.

Another group of non-Manipuri women comprises of Nepalis who are mainly rural based and who usually practice cultivation as a means of livelihood. Generally their educational attainments are lower than that of other non-Manipuri women, and many are employed as domestic maids. Their status can be illustrated in their demeanor towards their husbands. For instance a live-in maid who completes her work within a maximum of three to four hours, despite being allowed by her employee to go out for personal or recreational reasons, fears to do so, in case she is late in returning, and her husband who lives with her, but works elsewhere, returns to his quarter and finds her out, instead of waiting subserviently to receive him. There are a few affluent working Nepali women who enjoy a higher status, but their number is negligible.

Ethnic tradition in both the hills and plains emphasized the 'extreme' contribution of women in the subsistence economies. Independence of character and positive self reliant action by women often challenged the entrenched notion of essential domestication of the female and gave women intrinsic nuances of mobility and freedom[56]. Women have to pass through several phases of restraint to enter the men dominated public sphere. Here the questions of mobility and profession become important concerns in the public sphere, debated through the need of education for women. The

Gandhian strategy to include women in the national movement by maintaining the existing patriarchy, also helped a large section of the women to come out openly. The participation in the freedom movement gave a new meaning to women's public value[57]. However, Gandhi had qualified women's role: 'women leaders were essentially equal to men and had a right to freedom, liberty and a supreme place in their own sphere of activity, yet both sexes should follow different vocations suitable to their different physical and emotional temperaments'. The Gandhian solution remained incomplete—no viable alternative against the prevailing patriarchal structure and women's sub-ordination[58]. In Manipur during the colonial period (1891-1947) the women of Imphal vociferously protested the orders of the British for their menfolk to go to Tamu to collect wood to rebuild the house of the Political Agent. This protest was known as the 'First Nupilan' 1904. The Second Nupilan of 1939 was led by woman vendors of the Khwairamband Bazaar Imphal, to protest the artificial scarcity of rice caused by export of the same by the colonial authorities[59]. The most admirable feature of the Manipuri women has been their capacity to resist any imposition on them, their families or their state, be it in the social, political or economic field[60]. Women in Manipur, in fact, have been at the forefront of the movement for human rights and have led many social movements. Manipuri women's role in the socio-economic and cultural life of Manipur is significant. Manipuri women do not stay behind the veil[61].

The Second Nupilan was a spontaneous eruption of the suppressed energy of the exploited people. The main course of the movement was directly related to the irregularities and malpractices in the administration of the state, and the economic exploitation by the authority. The women campaigned against economic policies that permitted rice to be exported out of the kingdom at the cost of the ability of its own people to access food. For many months, the women who run the main bazaar in Imphal viz. the Khwairamband Bazaar, refused to operate their stalls. The Bazaar remained devastated for three years. Ultimately they succeeded in bringing reforms in administration. The outbreak of women's agitation was a turning point in the emergence of a new trend of political and national consciousness in the state[62]. As a result after Manipur became independent in 1947, Manipur women enjoyed the right to universal adult franchise in 1948.

Manipuri women played an active role in the 1954-55 movement for the restoration of the democratic government of 1948, and in the statehood movement of the 1960's. (Manipur became a state in 1972)[63]. Women continued in the exercise of their right to vote in Parliamentary as also Territorial Council elections, and after 1972 in elections to the State Legislative Assembly as also Parliament. Today, in a House of 60 elected representatives, three are women, but only one viz. Mira Bai holds a cabinet rank.

In fact Jananetta Irawat (1896-1951) had established a Vhadra Mahila Samaj (1933) and a Manipuri Mahila Sanmelong (1940). A woman T. Thoibi Devi was on the editorial board of the 'Anouba Yug' (1947) a weekly edited by him. The first woman candidate Tongbram Ningol Sabi Devi to the 1st Manipur Assembly Election 1948, was a member of the Manipur Krishak Sabha, a political organization formed under Irawat's leadership[64].

From the 1970's onwards, use of alcohol greatly escalated, and drunken violence against women, especially wives, posed a serious threat to the organization and well being of both family and society as a whole. Inebriated men who resorted to abuse at home, created a fear psychosis in their wives and children—moreover it impaired the capacity of such men to work. Women took the lead and formed collectives to check alcohol abuse—this movement came to be known as the Nisha Bandh movement. Women patrolled the streets at night and severely punished drunkards. Ironically, many of these same women weakly submitted to physical abuse by their drunken spouse in the private realm of the family, where they were deprived of the support of women's collectives. In the public domain their collective solidarity empowered them to the extent that they could severely reprimand abusers.

In the valley, women's activism is symbolized by the activities of the Meira Paibis who hold *mashaals*. They have become an institution in their own right. They campaign against atrocities by the security forces[65] and uphold human rights. In the hill areas of Manipur, there are a number of Naga women's organizations who work for improving the quality of life for women and also abolishing discriminatory customary practices, and introducing income generation programmes. The Kuki Women's organizations have similar goals and programmes and also facilitate peace among clans/tribes which are warring with one another. The Tangkhul Shanao Long is pro active in defending human rights for e.g. the protest against the eviction of residents of Naga river colony in Imphal (2013).

With changes in polity and the political landscape especially after Manipur attained statehood, women's groups became pro-active: champions of human rights especially on occasions of armed clashes between security forces and non state actors and also innocent civilians—they work tirelessly to prevent loss of life, disappearance of boys and men, rapes and other crimes against women. The whole state came to a standstill when a woman named Manorama Devi on grounds of mere suspicion, was allegedly raped and killed in 2004 by the Assam Rifles. To decry such a bestial crime, 12 brave women of Manipur undertook a 'naked' protest at the Gate of Kangla (the erstwhile capital which for many decades was occupied first by the British and then the Indian security forces) daring the army to kill/rape them. Such a protest was a first in the history not only of the women's movement, but also in the history of Manipur. It ushered in a sea-change in the attitude of the Assam Rifles who then embarked on a programme of civil actions—performing many duties which are the responsibility of the government such as provision of water facilities, educational aids, construction of roads/community halls, levelling of playgrounds etc.

It is seen that women's mobilization on a large scale has been a feature of identity politics. The frequent complaint that women are used as shields to protect men is true, but it is also true that the ethnic dress of the women makes the identification of the agitations easier. In the female dominated societies of the North East, women's labour provides the very substance of the communities existence as a group. The 'control' of women in identity politics based on ethnicity, such as mobilization of women for mass actions, imposition of dress codes (as in Manipur), no marriage with 'outsiders', is different from the control of women in a classical patriarchal set-up. Another burning gender issue in the context of identity politics and the rise of ethnic based movements is the issue of rape. Allegations of rape of ethnic women by armed personal representing the state machinery, and mobilizations on the issue of rape, have become a regular feature of identity politics in North East India. In the North East movements, women become counters in the political struggle for domination and subjugation, and rape gains added significance because of the greater sensitivity of North East communities to the label of promiscuity given to North East women by patriarchal Indian society. The response to Manorama's alleged rape and murder is significant of the deep resentment against such branding of immorality[66].

The status of Manipur women is closely linked to their economic role. The British ethnographers had unanimously agreed on the industriousness of the women. Because of Manipur's history of warfare prior to the advent of colonial rule, women had the responsibility of all transactions in the markets of Manipur. 'The habit of the country is to have bazaars at convenient spots by the roadside, where a handful of women congregate at an early hour. Imphal possesses the largest and the most important of the bazaars (Sana Keithel)[67]. Of it, is written: 'we are very proud of a South East Asian character in the existence of the women's market'[68]. In Muslim inhabited areas, markets are also held in the village square where groups of Muslim women would assemble, either in the morning or evening, selling groceries, and all the basic commodities which they amass from the adjoining villages. Miniature versons of Khwairamband Bazaar (the premier women's market) of Imphal can be seen in almost all the Muslim settlement areas[69]. Women vendors occupy regular stalls, just as Meitei women in the Khwairamband Bazaar (though these is a very little admixture of women from the Pangal and tribal communities) and sell everything required for daily necessities from food, clothing, bed linen, ornaments, etc. 'Apart from its economic significance the market serves as an important institution of social and political interaction'[70]. The local markets also play an important role in rural development. Besides providing service and outlets for rural produce—these markets ensure the efficiency of the food distribution system, and inter-community linkages[71].

Even today, women continue to operate the markets. Manipuri women are not only active, but 'experts in marketing their products'. Manipur is the only state having an exclusive 'Women's Market'. The daily market of Nupi Keithel has a population of more than 2000 women selling their own products: These women have continued their involvement in issues confronting Manipuri society[72], for instance in June 2013 they undertook a day long *dharna* demanding enforcement of the Inner Line Permit. Women had and have to face challenges to safeguard their market from the rival markets managed and controlled by men of varied Indian trading companies[73]. (The Women's market is in the centre of the two main markets—Thangal Bazar and Paona Bazar mainly run by male traders).

Despite the vibrancy and buoyancy of women's markets, the women vendors do not enjoy the privileges and security of traders/ businessmen in the formal sector of the economy. They have no health or accident insurance, no time off, no maternity benefits etc. The unlicensed women vendors, of which there are many in Imphal are constantly harassed by the police, and forced to run helter-skelter with their goods, which they normally display on pavements, and on the roadside, as they have not been allotted any permanent stalls in the women's market, despite the upper floods of the rebuilt women's Markets being vacant for many years. However, all too often, if they pay a cash bribe, the police turn their eyes away and allow them to ply their unlicensed trade.

Women's labour is certainly appreciated and recognized, but when viewed from another prism, it presents a dichotomy. 'We have been socially applauding the contribution the women have been making to make our economy survive,' but have we ever done anything to see that women are facilitated in their functioning?

We know that we have a strong presence of women in the larger daily socio-economic exchange of relations. Yet we witness them performing the natural urination functions in a corner because of the cumulative failure of our policy thinking to address the need of convenience rooms. We also know that our women are responsible for ensuring the availability of vegetables in the kitchens and clothes around our body, and for prayers, and what not. In order to perform this commendable economic function, they have been out of their homes with loads over their heads. The buses have been their only available medium of transportation for years. But have we even pondered on designing a bus to facilitate the movement of women playing the most important role in the socio-economic life of the land. All our buses are on borrowed designs, and based on economics very different from Manipur's[74]. Traffic policewomen are also deprived of washroom and toilet facilities during long hours of work.

The sphere of work is the one area where women's actual economic participation exceeds that of men in most cases. But most women work in the primary sector which provides mere subsistence; in the secondary sector, women are involved in informal home-based activities, which provide little financial or social security. Women's share in organized sector employment was 0.8 per cent in lakhs[75].

Majority of the women in Manipur are the bread earners in the family in many instances—the 'only' bread earners. Traditionally, the loom was a integral part of the gifts given to the daughter at her wedding. It is here that woman becomes a producer and later also a retailer, when she sells her creations in the markets. Women in the household industries outnumber the men (in Senapati district 2,530 women versus 924 men, Churachandpur district 5397 women versus 1646 men, Bishnupur district 9238 women versus 2157 men and Thoubal district 16,449 women versus 3,744 men). Among main workers, men outnumber women, but among marginal workers, women outnumber men. In the agricultural sector there are more men cultivators whereas in the more labour intensive and less paid job of agricultural labourers, women outnumber men. In the tertiary sector women occupying the Director's, Commissioner's, Secretary's post, are extremely few in number. In the lower rung of the office hierarchy, where there is not much challenge and scope, but is labour intensive there are women employees[76]. This despite the high sex ratio in Manipur 992 females per 1000 males (2011 census), higher than most other states. The paradox in women's status persists, a case study illustrates this: 'Mimi was married while she was still studying in class VIII. After she was raped by a boy, her in-laws refused to accept her. Mimi thought things would change if she had a baby. She gave birth to a son, yet her husband decided to remarry. Unable to bear the humiliation, she consumed poison (but was saved)[77].

Although there are several provisions in tribal customary law that promote gender equity, not all customary laws are gender sensitive. In most tribes, if a woman does not have a son, inheritance is near impossible. After the death of a husband, custody of children and property rights devolve to the in-laws. Women have no inheritance rights, and even if a father leaves properties in his daughter's name, the male cousins of the girl will claim them after the death of the father[78]. Valley Rose, a journalist stated: 'women were considered secondary citizens in society. Head counts are made of only male members. Women are not allowed to speak out in front of male folk. Women are excluded from the village Authority/Council'[79]. (There are a few exceptions—for example a Moyon woman became the Speaker of the assembly of the Moyon Naga Council in 1997. The President of the Moyon Sanuw Ruwrkheh (a women's organization) was also given the right to vote)[80]. Naga customary law excludes women from inheriting parental properties.

In Manipur, the term 'Ima' (mother) has a special connotation and is extolled on the public platform, but today hundreds, if not thousands of women continue to be a battered lot within the confines of their homes. Wife beating and domestic violence is a reality. In every sphere of life, women continue to be at the receiving end of the brutalities of menfolk, and what makes things more galling is the veil of social hypocrisy under which these bestial acts are carried out[81]. 'It is talked, mentioned and repeated day in and day out in Manipur, that the position of women is much safer and status much higher, than anywhere in the world. But the dynamics and contextual manifestations have turned out to be much degraded and anti-woman, contrary to the facial display of social functioning. There is now the fundamental urgency of appreciating the economics and the technological aspects of the entire dynamics. Young research scholars working on gender issues in Manipur have been arguing that the whole high status of women is only a hoax - to conveniently suppress their voice, and exploit their contribution to the advantage of the male. With so many reports of rapes and other crimes emerging, it only reinforces that there is point, in this argument[82]. Whereas one social activist states that women are revered in Manipuri society, another is of the opinion that women are commodified in men's consciousness. However, separated and divorced women do not suffer social discrimination as is common in dominant patriarchal societies, and they (Meiteis) have rights to natal and marital properties[83].

Manipur can also boast of having the lowest infant mortality rates which would mean that female infanticide is not prevalent, but in contrast the evil of the traditional Indian dowry system has taken root in the state, both in the valley and the hills. The awonpot of the Meiteis and the bride price of the tribals has now changed its form—expensive items, meant for display and enhancement of socio-economic status figure prominently at the time of the marriage of a girl. In addition some families try to resolve their debts by extracting a large cash dowry for their son's hand in marriage[84]. Other reasons for a cash dowry include money required by the groom's family for purposes of higher education abroad, construction of a house, etc.[85]. There are increasingly many instances reported by the print media of young women attempting/ committing suicide because of harassment by in-laws because of inability of the woman to provide a substantial dowry.

In contrast, Manipuri society honours women in a unique manner on the occasion of 'Ningol Chakouba'—a day set aside for fathers and brothers to invite their daughters and sisters to their natal home for a grand feast followed by presentation of gifts to the women. This is the one occasion when women really come into their own and enjoy the day. But paradoxically the food provided for the feast has to be prepared by the 'Ningols" (married women) in the marital residence-they then attire themselves in beautiful outfits and jewelry, and accompanied by their children go to their parents residence to enjoy the day. However they are required to return to their husband's residence before dark.

But despite the combination of Meira Paibis who agitate against threats to society and the maibis who give them spiritual support in the valley, despite the powerful tribal women's organizations both in the hills and the valley, all women irrespective of community are forced to multi task-the women is the first to rise and the last to go to bed. It is taken for granted that the woman must toil yet they are to be excluded from decision making apparent from the Thadou saying 'Numei leh chapang simlou,' exclude women and children. Of Paite women it is stated: 'they work day and night like a servant, yet there were rebuked and insulted.'[86] In a similar vein the Kukis use the sentence: Numei Phalou le honpal phalou chu khel ding mong ahi'—a bad wife and a bad fence can always be replaced[87]. Although Kuki Christian women undertake preaching tour i.e. Gambih, and the first woman pastor to be ordained from Manipur was Nemneikim Vaiphei in 1998, when the Rev. Kim got married in February 2003, there was great opposition from male Church leaders, as she had been ordained on the condition that she would remain single[88]. However celibacy is not enjoined on a male pastor. The lady Reverend subsequently left the Kuki Baptist Convention and joined the Methodist Church. However, a lot of people admire the Kuki women's way of life as not only unique but in conformity with high standards of morality[89]. Similarly, the Simte Law of Inheritance is discriminatory to women as it bars them from inheriting property. A widow can only use her husband's land and house during her lifetime[90].

In Naga society too, a woman has no share in land properties of her father or husband. But on the other hand Naga women were free from the evils of a 'dowry system, sati, *purdah*, child marriage, bride burning, female infanticide[91]. Bride price was also prevalent. In contrast, "women are prohibited from having any say in both social and family affairs in the Zeliangrong Naga society, because they believe that the presence of women in such affairs is a bad omen for the whole society. It is tabooed for a warrior to sleep with his wife, or even touch her inner clothes, before going to war, or for hunting[92].

Among the Mao, Paomei and Maram Naga, women join the war by standing behind the two warring groups. When the fighting becomes too severe women intervene by stepping forward. Naga customary law forbids harming women, and the women's action results in a declaration of peace. This women's intervention is unique and a tribute to Naga women[93]. It is also the duty of a husband's family to protect a young wife after the marriage. If the husband wife relationship is strained, and there is no other alternative other than divorce, it is duty of the bride's parents to ask their daughter to return home[94] so a divorced wife enjoys a certain security.

The Boy's or Bachelor's dormitory is strictly taboo for women. As A.C. Haddon states: 'these places are tabooed to women' they are used as dwelling or meeting places of men; they constitute the social, political and religious centres in the public life of men[95]. The logic is that if women were allowed into the dormitories ill luck would befall men. After the rape of L. Rose by the BSF and her subsequent suicide, the Tangkhul leaders desired that women's organizations come into existence, and on the 8th May 1974, the East District Women's Association was formed to protect and fight for the rights and dignity of women so as to bring about development, justice and peace. The Tangkhul Women's Long (Union) acts as a watchdog to prevent VAW. Today it is one of the strongest bodies of Tangkhul women; all Tangkhul women are members, and each has a role to pay in reforming society and protecting it[96].

Although Naga women are excluded from the Village Council, the apex political body of the Nagas, 'in politics and diplomacy, women could influence in many ways, directly or indirectly the village councilors, though their husband or their father', and as a neutral party intervene in war. There were times when women assumed the mantle of leadership e.g. Mrs. Hinga Karangnmei who exercised the power of Chief (Sangungpui) in Maram Khullen in Senapati district after the death of her husband. Similar instances are cited with reference to the Moyon and Tangkhul tribes too. A Tangkhul woman Harkhongla of Maram village was elected to the village council and was the commander-in-chief during war in her village. Other women leaders were Kaireila of Talui who participated in deliberations of the village council, Shakhala of Mangchon, Seikhangla of Laotei, Lamengla of Tuinem. Outstanding among the Zeliangrong community was Rani Gaidinliu who fought alone 'to preserve the culture, and to bring back the past glory'. She stimulated political awareness not only among Zeliangrong women but other women of Manipur. Some Kabui Naga women have been elected as Councilors to the Imphal Municipal bodies and Gram Sabhas as a result of the 73rd Amendment (Reserving one-third seats for women in Panachayat Raj institutions)[97]. A remarkable achievement following on the heels of Manipur's independence in 1947 was the election of Mrs. Hangmila Shaiza to the Manipur Territorial Legislative Assembly. In recent times, other Naga women have contested in the assembly elections unsuccessfully.

Although Kuki women's groups are not as effective as the Naga groups because they lack both cohesion and unity, and the focus of their attention is short-lived (as for instance, their attempt to patrol the villages for the purpose of keeping the village safe from drunkards and other anti-social elements their efforts never lasted beyond one calendar year), a few Kuki women entered early in the domain of politics as for e.g. Akim Anal and Lhingjaneng Gangte in 1958 and 1962 as members of the Territorial Council, whereas Kim Gangte was the first woman to be elected as a Member of Parliament in 1998. Nemcha Kipgen was elected to the State Assembly in 2012—the first Kuki woman to be elected to the assembly. Three women have been elected as members of

Autonomous District Councils in 2010, and one other, Lewish Sitlhou was nominated to the Sadar Hills Autonomous District Council as early as 1974[98].

Among the Meiteis, as early as 1952, M.K. Binodini was elected to the Electoral College, Ishwari Devi contested the parliamentary election but lost. So also Shabi Devi was defeated in the Territorial Council Elections in 1957. But R.K. Mukhra Devi and A. Bimola Devi were nominated to the Territorial Assembly 1963-69. After a gap of three decades, K. Apabi Devi was elected to the state assembly in 1992 and in 2000, W. Leima Devi. The latter won again in 2002. In 2007, Landhoni Devi wife of the present Chief Minister was elected, and in the most recent election (2012) she along with A.K. Mirabai was elected; A.K. Mirabai going on to become a Cabinet Minister. Under the constitutional provisions of reserving seats for women, Meitei women have found a place in municipal bodies and gram panchayats. However all too often, these women are influenced by men especially their male relatives in making decisions on important matters, partly because those elected from reserved seats are uneducated, and simultaneously do not realize the importance of actively participating in the political process at the grassroots level. They have also been socially conditioned to abide by the decisions of their menfolk. Finding lack of women's participation in the village council, the youth of Sirarakhong village, Ukhrul district passed a resolution to include women in decision making e.g. women of Tungjoy village, Senapati district are invited to and consulted by the village council. The same practice is followed by Naga churches[99]. In Naga society, two factors acted as a catalyst to empower women-the Naga political Movement and the movement to prevent VAW by the armed forces. 'The leaders of the Naga Nationalists called for every Naga man and woman to join hands to work for national rights and freedom, many women joined the movement as soldiers, nurses, teachers and so on'[100]. The journalist Valley Rose describes women's participation: 'Naga women have always taken an active part in their people's struggle to maintain or protect their rights to self-determination and against social evils in society'.

In religion, Kabui Naga women have special roles, as for examples in the Banru sacrifices to God. Mao women before commencing rice plantation perform a ceremony to propitiate the spirits of the paddy fields. They also have to perform Koyu (depating ceremony) for a deceased husband. In addition during the 'Feast of Merit', it is the wife who blesses the wooden vats of wine before distribution to the villages. Women also perform a ritual associated with Chumpha Phanit to the Goddess of Wealth—after that only can Tangkhuls eat the 'new rice' (freshly harvested). Barring a few sacrifices, women actively participate in religious ceremonies—propitiation of household deity, ancestral, village and the Supreme Deity[101].

After conversion to Christianity, women's societies were established in all churches, women were appointed both as deacons and trustees, and a lady Shinmingla was appointed Pastor of Bungpa Khunou Baptist Church from 1942 to 1949, and another Sanrengla as Pastor of Nambisha Baptist Church 1944[102]. This was a revolutionary measure in the history of the Baptist Church in Manipur. However information on their pastoral tenure is unavailable and a comparative analysis with male pastors is not possible.

Despite the dichotomy in the status of Manipuri women, there are some outstanding women who have brought admiration and laurels to the state. The first of these remarkable women is Irom Sharmila, a Meitei woman who began on an indefinite fast from November 2000 to protest the killing of innocent people by security forces-the incident is known in history as the 'Malom Massacre'. Upto date, she continues her fast, the longest in human history—demanding the removal of the Armed Forces Special Power Act (AFSPA) which provides impunity to security personnel from prosecution. She has decided to sacrifice 'normal' life—by refusing to accept status quo, her sacrifice speaks louder than words insisting: it is not normal for ordinary people to be killed in the name of law and order, it is not normal for us to look the other way, when innocent people are killed in the name of justice by a state that claims to be a democracy, it is not normal to ignore the violations and just get on with one's own life[103]. She began her fast at the young age of twenty eight years, and stands as a beacon of hope and courage to all women, especially those subjected to VAW by security forces. She will give up her fast as soon as AFSPA is withdrawn. Her determined protest against AFSPA has won the admiration not only of women, but all sections of the population and has encouraged many women, young and old, to become activists and demand their rights. Her form of protest as also the nude protest by women following Manorama's death (2004), 'have used the power of the human body to mould, formulate and transmit messages, communicating important truths[104].

Apart from Sharmila, there are outstanding women, remarkable for their individual achievements in different walks of life. Another such role model is a young tribal sportswoman viz. Mary Kom, the Olympic Bronze Medalist (2012) in boxing. Her achievement is all the more remarkable in that she battled against all odds to become a world champion, to bring laurels to the state and country. She stands out as a shining example—conveying through her achievements, the message that 'where there is a will, there is a way', and even impoverished or marginalized women can come into their own if they possess the right spirit and determination.

Manipur with its rich cultural heritage, has produced world famous dancers, singers, litterateur, sportspersons, martial art experts from the ranks of women in society. The recent achievement of a young woman of Manipur viz. N. Bidyapati Devi scaling Mount Everest in June 2012 is a case in point. And despite the lack of law and order, some young women have become successful business entrepreneurs in their own right.

There are a sizable section of women who are respected because of their personal achievements in the various branches of government service, IAS, IPS, IFS, MCS (Manipur Civil Service) officers, judges, lawyers, doctors, health professionals, academicians, educationists, hoteliers and a host of others. And there are remarkable women who whether suffering from HIV or cancer, are living life meaningfully, and even pursuing a career.

But these women form only a small minority. Despite the female sex ratio in Manipur being 992 females to a 1000 males (2011 census) woman as a whole do not enjoy an equal status with men, even though some of them have acquired property in their own right, whereas some have inherited or received a part of ancestral property. A glaring disparity is that although a vast majority of women from different communities in Manipur are engaged day in and day out in the pursuit of a sustainable livelihood, most of them are outside the umbrella of an organized, recognized labour force. They are deprived of benefits like mandatory holidays, leisure time, sick or maternity leave, annual holidays, insurance and provident fund benefits. But 'a woman in Meitei society (at least), is indeed a recognized citizen of the community by virtue of her own identity as a member of the 'Khulang' (rice cultivation team), Marup (credit association), Nupi Pala (women's religious association), and various other activities, regardless of her marital status. Tribal women enjoy more mobility and freedom. 'The position of women in North-East society is different in comparison to those living in other parts of India. Women enjoy greater mobility and visibility, than women of other communities in the country. The more egalitarian tribal culture of the North-East region, coupled with the absence of some rigid practices prevalent in other parts of India, like *purdah* and dowry, certainly gives women of the region an edge over other women, in terms of rights. The concept of solidarity amongst women's groups is fairly strong. Violence that women face at the domestic level is fairly less as compared to those residing in the rest of the country[105]. However, a woman poet pained by the restrictions imposed on women by patriarchy in Manipur writes:

> 'You drenched the earth with your own blood,
> You aroused waves of excitement with you smiles,
> But you remained neglected,
> Known to none
> Woman, O Woman!
> Whoever are you?[106]

Another poetess protests the restrictions placed on women:

> Don't confine me here
> Open the door and let me out
> If you keep it closed
> I'll force myself through
> By breaking open
> The seven bolted door[107]

But a very telling poem on the fate that awaits a married woman is Memchoubi's 'On My Wedding Day'

> The relatives, aged womenfolk,
> My mother, my grandma,
> Aunts, nieces, and dames,
> Tiptoeing in endless succession
> On my wedding day,
> All had their say.
> In a pitiful tone did they chorus,
> It is sacrilege for daughters
> To die in parental homes
> And so—
> Though ill treated, though loveless,
> Though circumscribed with utter pains,
> Endure you must, and remain so,
> Never towards this place
> Must your face turn up.
> Never again in the least
> Are you allowed to be back[108].

Hearing such advice/exhortation, which bride would want to leave her natal home?

And describing tribal married woman's plight, R.R. Gangmei wrote 'Most tribal married women cannot be considered beauties. Their faces darken with 'mahing' (toiling in torrential rain and scorching heat with an infant on her back, a toddler crying incoherently—they are not tanned but sunburnt irrevocably). A thirty year old mother looks twenty years older than her age[109].

A male social activist while stating that 'women are revered in Manipuri society', goes on to say that crimes against women had not been heard off until 1980. But a woman activist asserts that these crimes are caused by the common mindset of commoditization of women embedded in men's consciousness[110]. This last statement is made explicit in the action of four IRB (Indian Reserve Battalion) jawans, who were arrested by Churachandpur Police in connection with forcibly video recording two lovers in the nude and uploading it on a social networking site—the nude picture went viral. Although the ethics of moral policing is questionable, what happened near Khuga Dam in Churachandpur district a few days back reveals the perverted mindset of four men in uniform. Adopting a high moral standard cannot get more twisted and alarming than this. In uploading the video clip on the net, the young Churachandpur girl must have died a hundred times. The behaviour of the young girl—making out in the woods is not acceptable[111] but what is reprehensible is the action of security personnel in filming explicitly the couple's action and then making the pictures public.

These is also a small minority of women who through their own actions lower the status of women. Incidents have occurred where a group of young, attractive enterprising women, indulge in immoral actions to earn a fast buck—they literally trap eligible men into marriages, temporary not permanent. They plan strategies to force a man to elope with one of them (elopement has social sanction in the state). Immediately following the elopement, the girls family files a case of forcible abduction in a nearby police station. This is followed by negotiations between the families of the boy and girl. As the boy is regarded as a culprit, his family have to cough up a substantial sum of money to get the case withdrawn. The monetary gain comes to the girl's family or more explicitly—the girl who planned the elopement. There are of course others who benefit as well—the police personnel who are in the know-how. Some of these women indulging in the practice are supposedly infected with HIV. Perhaps to earn money for ART drugs, or because of poverty and unemployment, they resort to such unsavoury practices. Such instances have been reported (not publicly) from Moirang.

Some activists are of the opinion that Manipuri women who marry non-Manipuris, must forfeit the right to inheritance of land/ property and be barred from purchasing land in Manipur in their own names—this discrimination is a reflection of women's lower status. And despite the absence of female infanticide, the child sex ratio of the state as per the 2011 census is 936 girls for a 1000 boys[112].

On Hmar women, Priyadarshini M. Gangte writes: Traditional institutions and customary laws among tribal people portray an egalitarian socio-economic structure, which is in fact discriminatory when it comes to women's right in traditional governance and customary law. Socio-cultural values push women into a closed domestic domain, burdened by mundane, but extremely strenuous economic activity. The researcher Bonita stated 'The male dominated Hmar society was not the root cause, for oppression of women—it was the continuity of tradition. Women themselves rejected the idea of being independent and having a separate identity. The Hmar women despite their access to education, remain a closely bound patriarchal society, confined by rules and tested[113].

Another factor associated with woman's status, is the ability of a women to operate her bank account independently and keep it confidential. However, many women are forced to operate in secret, because of continuous demands on their income/salary. On a recent visit to a bank, a change of attitude on the part of female bank officers and staff is discernible. A gentleman made an enquiry to a woman officer about his wife's bank account—the latter politely but categorically replied that his wife's account was confidential, and details could not be divulged by her. Many women who are full time housewives want their daughters to be financially independent and pursue their own careers. One such woman recently separated from her husband because though the husband was also an earner, he expected his wife who was a salaried individual, to pay for the upkeep and maintenance of the house and the education of their child. This is not a solitary instance—many men who boast of their wives respectable jobs, expect them to expend all their income on home and family. And these same men rarely pay for a vacation for their wives, or give them occasional gifts whether expensive or not, such as flowers, or take them out for a meal in a restaurant. The last is operative largely when the young man is trying to win favour with a woman. Once married, there is no requirement to woo her in a restaurant or give her a gift.

Because of an increase in literacy (literacy rate of women in Manipur is 72.4) and the phenomena of rural-urban migration, working women especially have little free time. Rural migrant women have no desire to work as maids or domestic helpers, because education especially in the case of tribal women makes them capable of getting better qualified jobs, and moreover the salary of maids is generally low and they too enjoy little leisure time. So a young working urban woman has to juggle her work on the various fronts—family, (especially children) home and office—the result is that by the end of each day she is really hard put to stay awake and enjoy even watching TV or surfing the Net. Many women consciously or unconsciously (because they have been conditioned) sacrifice for their families, and spend more on family obligations rather than on financial security[114]. There are many instances when adult children literally force working mothers to allow them to use the latter's ATM debit card—they then withdraw to the maximum limit, leaving the mother the bare minimum. Its easier for them to strong-arm mothers, rather than fathers. But with the emergence of nuclear families, a widow or a divorcee may find herself in dire financial straits. Her woes may be compounded, if she is elderly and suffers from Alzheimer's, and cannot afford a full time care giver, sometimes even a part-time caregiver. (Alzheimer seems to be a common ailment affecting a large number of older women in Manipur). A women's grown-up children may not have the time and sometimes even the desire to lend support—moral, emotional, physical or financial because of their own work and responsibilities. So an elderly woman who may have commanded great respect in her prime, is left in her twilight years to fend for herself largely. Very recently some awareness has been created about Alzheimer's.

The replacement of 'awonpot' (traditional gifts given to the bride) by a substantial dowry has also lowered women's status, in that a lot of brides are judged by the assets they bring with them to their marital home in the form of cash, gold ornaments, electronics, automobiles etc. If the assets are regarded as too meagre, the young women are harassed and taunted and many of them in desperation commit suicide or at least attempt to do so.

Rural especially hill women who do not migrate, but whose children respond to the pull of urbanization, are deprived of their assistance not only in household chores (the daughters) but in essential work of cultivation. There are no statistics available on money, remitted by such children to their mothers at home; when income declines there is also a proportionate decline in social status. A woman bank officer asserted that it is a one way transaction—money only goes out of the state to fund children's education, expensive lifestyle, etc.

And in the famed Women's Market, despite the autonomy of women vendors, the majority have a difficult time earning enough for themselves and their family. As a result of both consumerism and globalization, cheap manufactured goods are flooding other markets of the state, and many of these goods especially those coming through Myanmar are much more popular and in demand. The Ima markets that sell indigenous textiles are adversely impacted, this is exacerbated by the fact that such products produced in conditions of individual labour without the use of modern technology are very highly priced in comparison to the low priced, attractive goods coming especially from countries of South East and East Asia.

Feminist historian Gerder Lerner stated that patriarchy originated with the establishment of the earliest states, and ever since then, the state has been the main instrument for institutionalizing gender and caste/class based structures of exploitation and domination. The historical process is underwritten by the unacknowledged and unseen labour of women and the subject classes. In the case of women, the labour was both productive and reproductive. The crucial factor in patriarchal systems is the control of women[115]. Rekha Roy states: Feminists in recent times believe that patriarchy signified the cultural and social domination of women by men. Most feminists believe that attitudes towards women are a socio-cultural construct and can change—not merely with political and legal actions—social actions at the family stage should happen before these attitudes change[116]. She adds: Although the Constitution guarantees the same legal status to women as men, most women are poor, and this effectively bars them from decision-making, even in purchasing cheap birth control measures especially Manipuri Muslim women. Moreover, women's workload, despite new technology in the form of labour saving devices remains heavy. Even salaried or self-employed women perform all household chores as upto date, there is no equitable domestic division of labour between the sexes. The patriarchal element continues to predominate. Although under Equal Remuneration Act 1976, male and female workers receive the same wages, in practice, poor women workers are unable to prevent employees from discriminating against them[117].

In order to have a clear understanding of women's status it is imperative to consider women's role as also her responsibilities, and the hours of work she puts in daily as also her control over resources and her participation in decision making, as also the amount of leisure time she enjoys.

However, it is also important to analyse the role and contribution of the Meira Paibi movement in today's context, as they have played a significant role in the women's movement. They for long shouldered the responsibility of defending human rights. The use of 'Meira' as a weapon symbolizes the declaration of a just war. The use of fire, a sacred symbol of the Meiteis, adds sanctity to the movement[118]. But the ever increasing number of women's organizations (mostly funded) have made inroads into the voluntary work of the Meira Paibi, especially as funded women's NGO's focus on capacity building, skills training, sustainable livelihood, which assume cardinal importance in a liberalized economy. Moreover, funded NGO's pay their women staff a decent wage, and stipends are given at times of orientation programmes and workshops, as also travel allowances.

References

1. E.W. Dun, *Gazetteer of Manipur*, p. 17.
2. T.C. Hodson, *The Meitheis*, p. 23.
3. *The Sangai Express Editorial*, 30th April 2013.
4. The 'Cheitharol Kumpapa' or Royal Chronicle commences with the accession of Pakhangba to the throne of Manipur in 33 A.D.
5. L. Basanti, *Position of Women in Early Manipuri Society*, p. 163 cit. in Proceedings of North East India History Association, Jagiroad, 1991.
6. Lokendra Arambam, *Women and Public Causes*, Study of Meira Paibee of Manipur.
7. Arambam Ongbi Memchoubi, The Indigenous Meitei Women cit. in *Quarterly Journal*, No. 23, Feb. 2007, Manipur State, Kala Academy.
8. L. Basanti, *op. cit.*
9. N. Jayshree Devi, *History of Women's Education in Manipur upto 1947*, p. 60.
10. *Ibid.*, p. 63 cit. Dr. Konsom Manikchand-Anganba Matamgi Meitei Nupigi Phibam in *Sanathong* 1999, Vol. 5, p. 9.
11. *Ibid.*, p. 63.
12. Chunkham Sheelarani, Gender Construction in Meitei Society, pp. 34-35 cit. in *Quarterly Journal*, *op. cit.*
13. Ksh. Bimola Devi, *The Changing Role of Manipuri Women*, pp. 19-24, *op. cit.*
14. L. Basanti, *op. cit.*
15. Lokendra Arambam, *op. cit.*
16. N. Jayshree Devi, *op. cit.*, p. 32 cit. M. Chandra Singh (ed) Panthoibi Khongkul Reprint, Manipur Sahitya Parishad, Imphal, 1987, p. 3.
17. *Ibid*, cit. Dr. Budha Singh, *Indigenous Games of the Meitei*, Manipur, 1992 pp. 95-96.
18. *Ibid*, pp. 66-67.
19. Lokendra Arambam, *op. cit.*
20. L. Basanti, *op. cit.*
21. Arambam Ongbi Memchoubi, *op. cit.*
22. N. Jayshree Devi *op. cit.*, p. 32 cit. Memchoubi, Wakma Maibi, Writers Forum, Imphal 1999, pp. 9-15 (Wakma-bard).

23. Lokendra Arambam, *op. cit.*
24. S. Samson, Traditional Clan/Kinship/Customs and Relations with Reference to Women in Different Communities of Manipur.
25. Manjusri Chaki-Sircar, *Feminism in a Traditional Society*, p. 64.
26. Venetia Salam—Violence Against Women in Manipur–unpublished M.A. dissertation, King's College, London, 2012, p. 28 cit. *Grimwood, My Three Years in Manipur*, 1975, pp. 58-59.
27. N. Jayshree Devi, *op. cit.*, pp. 42-43, cit. Saroj Nalini Arambam Paratt (Translated) The Court Chronicle of the Kings of Manipur. The Cheitarol Kumpapa, London and New York, 2005, p. 47 and W. Lukhoi, Lai Haraoba, Manipur State Kala Akademi, Manipur, 1989, p. 21.
28. Field Study.
29. N. Jayshree Devi, *op. cit.*, p. 30, cit. Memchoubi-Amaibi-Manipur da Shamanism Arambam Yoimayai, 2006, p. 105.
30. *Ibid.*, cit. N. Ibochouba (ed) Thirel Layat, Imphal, 1981, p. 9.
31. *Ibid.*, cit., Khulen Chandrasekhar Singh (ed) Sakok Lamlen Ahanba, Imphal, 1992, p. 5.
32. S. Samson, *op. cit.*
33. Tingneichong Gangte, *Women's Role in 20th Century Manipur*, p. 200 cit. Raisunriang (news link) Naga Women's Union, Manipur, III Issue, October 1997, p. 10.
34. Venetia Salam *op. cit.*, p. 28 cit. Johnstone J., *Manipur and Naga Hills*, 1993.
35. Venetia Salam, Johnstone J., *Manipur and Naga Hills*, 1993, p. 28.
36. Furer Haimendorf C. Jon, *The Naked Nagas*, London, 1939.
37. S. Samson, *op. cit.*
38. Budha Kamei, Traditional Social System of Zeliangrong cit. in. *The Sangai Express*, May 2013.
39. R.R. Shimray, *Origin and Culture of the Nagas*, 1985, p. 169, Ven 9. 28.
40. Tingneichong Gangte, *op. cit.*, pp. 190-191.
41. Arfina Haokip, Position of Women in the Kuki Society, A Historical Study p. 1 and 4. Unpublished Ph. D. Thesis, Manipur University, 2013.
42. Carey and Tuck, *The Chin Hills*, Vol. 1., p. 189.
43. Arfina Haokip, *op. cit.*, p. 24, cit. K.J. Khothang and H.K. Khenthang A Brief Introduction to Tribal Language and Culture of the Paite.
44. *Ibid*, cit. A.S. Diamond, *Primitive Law, Past and Present*, London, 1971 p. 225.
45. Tingneichong Gangte, *op. cit.*, p. III.
46. T.S. Gangte, *The Kukis of Manipur*, p. 95.
47. Arfina Haokip, *op. cit.*, p. 26.
48. Tingneichong Gangte, *op. cit.*, p. 107, cit. G. Khamkam, *Manipur Past and Present*, Vol. 3, edited by N. Sanajaoba, p. 297.

49. S. Samson, *op. cit.*
50. Salam Irene, *The Muslims of Manipur*, p. 132.
51. *Ibid.*, p. 144, p. 182.
52. Md. Ahmad Ali Shah, *A Brief Historical Study of Religion and Society of the Pangals of Manipur.*
53. Madhu Rajput, *Social, Economic and Political Status of Women in Manipur*, p. 458-459 cit. Arun Irengbam-Between the Lines: Stereotypes and Prejudices, Opinion–I in *Manipur Update*, January 2000.
54. Rita Kamei, *Historical Study of Muslim Women in Manipur*, p. 111.
55. Syed Ahmed, *Women Empowerment and Development: A Case Study of Manipuri Muslim Women*, p. 12.
56. Lokendra Arambam, *op. cit.*
57. Bipul Chaudhury, Women and the Question of Assamese Nationalism in Colonial Assam, pp. 232-233 in *Souvenir*, NEIHA 2008.
58. *Ibid.*, p. 234.
59. Ksh. Bimola Devi, The Changing Role of Manipuri Women in *Quarterly Journal*, *op. cit.*, pp. 19-24.
60. Madhu Rajput, *op. cit.*, p. 466.
61. Ranjana Mishra, Gender Equality and Status of Manipur Women, pp. 547-548 in Editor Madhu Rajput, *Social and Cultural Stratification in North East India.*
62. *Ibid.*
63. Ksh. Bimola Devi, *op. cit.*, p. 28.
64. Arambam Ongbi Memchoubi, *op. cit.*, p. 12.
65. Nandini Basistha, *Women Managing Conflict*, p. 492 in Editor Madhu Rajput, *op. cit.*
66. Aparna Mahanta, *Understanding Politics of Identity and Ethnicity in the North East: A Gender Perspective*, p. 244-247 cit. in *Souvenir*, North East History Association, 2008.
67. T.C. Hodson, *op. cit.*, p. 23.
68. Amar Yumnam, Issue of Position of Women: Need for Contextualised Rethink cited in the *The Sangai Express*, 31st March 2012.
69. Salam Irene, *The Muslims of Manipur*, *op. cit.*, p. 143.
70. *Ibid.*, cit. Syed Ahmed, *Status of Muslim Women in Manipur*, p. 55.
71. *Ibid.*, p. 144.
72. Ranjana Mishra, *op. cit.*, p. 548.
73. Madhu Rajput, *op. cit.*, p. 461.
74. Venetia Salam *op. cit.*, p. 14 cit. Amar Yumnam, Issue of Position of Women — Need for Contextualized Rethink, cited in *The Sangai Express*, 31st March 2012.
75. Salam Irene, *Women Today* 1975-2003, Seminar Paper MAKHAIS 2003.
76. N. Vijaylakshmi Brara, A Situational Analysis of Women and Girls in Manipur, p. 22.

77. Madhu Rajput, *op. cit.*, p. 467.
78. Esther Chinnu, Violence against Women in Manipur, p. 60 cit. in ed. H. Sudhir, Jubita Hajarimayum, *Violence Against Women in North East India*.
79. N. Vijaylakshmi Brara, The Seen and Unseen, p. 92 cit. in *op. cit.*
80. Nadini Basistha, Women Managing Conflict, A Case Study of Manipur, p. 494 in Ed. Madhu Rajput, *op. cit.*
81. *The Sangai Express* Editorial, 27th March 2012.
82. Amar Yumnam, *op. cit.*
83. Venetia Salem *op. cit.*, p. 28 cit. A. Pinto, H. Jubita, *Community Response to Violence Against Women in Manipur*.
84. K. Ruhini Kumar Sharma, Th. Jayantakumar and S. Sanatomba, Female Foeticide in India with Special Reference to the North East cit. M. Natrajan, Victimisation of Women: A Theoretical Perspective in Proceedings of the North East India History Association, Kokrajahar, 2005.
85. *Ibid.*, *op. cit.*
86. Khamkan G. cit. in *Manipur Past and Present*, Vol. 3, ed. Naorem Sanajaoba, p. 297.
87. Tingneichong Gangte, *op. cit.*, p. 113.
88. *Ibid.*, *op. cit.*, p. 168.
89. *Ibid.*, *op. cit.*, p. 174.
90. Ginneihching, The History and Culture of the Simte Tribe in Manipur, pp. 125, 127.
91. V. Free Paothing, Status of Tangkhul Women, p. 7.
92. Tingneichong Gangte, *op. cit.*, p. 184, cit. Dr. Hunibou Newmai, The Role of Women in Zeliangrong Society, in *Women in Naga Society* edited by Dr. Lucy Zehol, p. 44.
93. Tingneichong Gangte, *op. cit.*, p. 187.
94. R. Simon, Social Structure and Rise of Middle Class Among the Manipur Tangkhul Naga Tribe, p. 23. Unpublished Ph.D. Thesis, Manipur University, 2012.
95. *Ibid.*, *op. cit.*, p. 26, cit. A.C. Haddon, Report of the Cambridge Anthropological Expedition to the Torres Straits, Vol. V, London ,1937, p. 78.
96. *Ibid.*, *op. cit.*, pp. 75-76.
97. Tingneichong Gangte, *op. cit.*, pp. 192-195.
98. Arfina Haokip, *op. cit.*, pp. 5-6.
99. Tingneichong Gangte, *op. cit.*, pp. 196-197.
100. Z.V. Paothing p. 70, Status of Tangkhul Women cit. in. Tingneichong Gangte, *op. cit.*, p. 197.
101. Tingneichong Gangte, pp. 214-220, *op. cit.*

102. *Ibid.*, pp. 222, 224.
103. Deepti Priya Mehrotra, Burning Bright Irom Sharmila, Preface, p. XIV.
104. *Ibid.*, *op. cit.* p. 97.
105. Swati Thakur, Insurgency Aftermath—Devastation for Women, p. 503 in Madhu Rajput, Editor *op. cit.*
106. Memchoubi, Wherever are you, 1984 cit. in N. Aruna, Feminism in Manipuri Poetry, p. 62, cit. in *Quarterly Journal*, *op. cit.*
107. Kshetrimayum Subadini, Peegi, Wari, The Tale of Tears, 1995, cit. in N. Aruna, *op. cit.*, p. 71.
108. Memchoubi: On my Wedding Day, Translated by M. Priyobrata Singh, p. 87, *Quaterly Journal op. cit.*
109. R.R. Gangmei, Who to Blame cit. in *The Sangai Express*, 10th May 2012.
110. *The Sangai Express*, 21st June, 2012.
111. *Ibid.*, Editorial, 2nd July, 2013.
112. Y. Thamkishore Singh IAS, Census of India, 2011, Manipur Series 15, p. ix.
113. Priyadarshini M. Gangte, Reflections on Hmar Women, Social Deprivation, Inheritance: An Analysis cited in *The Sangai Express*, 5th Dec. 2012.
114. Celine Augustine, *op. cit.*, p. 169.
115. Aparna Mahanta, *op. cit.*, p. 240.
116. Rekha Roy, Women's Rights in India: A Feminist Perspective, p. 82.
117. *Ibid.*, *op. cit.*, p. 93.
118. Yenning, Is the Meira Paibi Movement Facing Extinction, *The Sangai Express*, Sept. 15, 2013.

3

Vulnerability of Women

Its Causes

When one subscribes to the view that the status of women in Manipur is very high, the question arises as to why women are then vulnerable to all forms of violence. The obvious answer would be that Manipur is a state in conflict. To what does this conflict owe its origins?

When India became independent in 1947, so did Manipur, because prior to her defeat in the Anglo-Manipur War of 1891, Manipur was a monarchical state. Manipur was an ancient kingdom, a cradle of human civilization and creativity, which has come under the influence of many cultures of different ethnic groups who came at different times, and contributed to the growth of the civilization of Manipur. Manipur, being a gateway of India to South East Asia, was influenced by her geographic situation and ecology in the shaping of her history and cultural development. It also possesses a rich tradition of recorded history in the form of royal and family chronicles.[1] A legislative Assembly and a Council of ministers started functioning under the Manipur Constitution Act of 1947 after duly conducting elections under universal adult franchise. However, with the merger of Manipur as a part of India in 1949, the nascent democracy was summarily dissolved.[2]

This merger has popularly been described as a 'forced merger'. It generated great discontent, and was regarded as 'unconstitutional'. This discontent grew apace because for long decades, no development 'per se' took place in Manipur. Today, Manipur is so far behind in development that it can be regarded as the least developed state in the country. This neglect gave rise to a feeling of deprivation and loss, it led to the rise of resistance movements which transformed into open armed conflict from the 1970's onwards[3]. Another factor for conflict was the imposition of AFSPA. It was in August 1958 when the Armed Forces (Assam and Manipur) Special Powers Bill was introduced in the Lok Sabha, the two lone MP's from Manipur-LaishramAchou and RungsungSaisa opposed the bill tooth and nail but to no avail. The then Union Home Minister Mr. G.B. Pant justified the bill, arguing that 'the local government may make use of the army, if it so chooses, in the manner provided in the Bill, and can use the army only for this limited purpose, and thereafter, the ordinary processes of law are to be followed'.[4] In the very first place, AFSPA has been in operation in Ukhrul for a period of three months with effect from 07-10-1960, and secondly in Tamenglong subdivision for a period of three months with effect from 27-5-1963. Since the 8th September 1980, the whole of Manipur state was declared a 'Disturbed State'.[5]

It is publicly acknowledged that in any area of conflict it is women who are more greatly impacted adversely, being vulnerable to all forms of violence. Conflict itself is a highly intricate phenomenon-only symptoms are observable, causes lie buried deep. The major cause and also effect of conflict is 'violence', both direct and structural. Direct violence maybe a personal attack on another, individual, physically, mentally or materially. Structural violence is a situation in which certain individuals are so influenced that their actual somatic and mental realization are below their potential capacity. Whether direct or structural, violence does create a situation for conflicts in society.[6] And women are the soft targets in any conflict situation. They easily become the first targets of both state and non-state actors because they are seen as the cultural identity of the group.[7] Women are used by state and non-state actors in different ways during conflict and in the practice of militarism without being conscious of it.[8] A visible direct result of conflict is women being caught in crossfire between armed groups, or being accused of siding with non state actors. Indirect result is an increase in widows–widows tend to be even more vulnerable and are often discriminated against.

Another reason for discontent is that Manipur became a state as late as 1972. And her language and script received recognition even later. In Manipur, as in other states in the North-East, there is an on-going struggle by people trying to establish their right to autonomy. The movement takes violent turns—army operations intensify the violence. The social disadvantage and subordination of women on the one hand, and the rapid socio-cultural and economic changes on the other hand significantly altered traditional structures and institutions within society. Such changes are inevitably associated with social upheaval. Political unrest has created difficult conditions for the different communities. New opportunities are either not materializing or are getting blocked.[9] Moreover, the insurgent groups involved in the armed struggle represent the various ethnicities inhabiting the state, leading to a complex interplay of identity politics along ethnic lines. The outlawed groups, numbering over thirty, are perhaps the highest of any Indian state. Each group has its own ideology, objectives and views, but one of the common grounds they share is secessionism. The Shukla Commission (1997) identified four deficits that created unrest and insurgencies—basic needs deficits, an infrastructural deficit, a resource deficit, and a two way deficit of understanding with the rest of the country.[10] These deficits, fifteen years along the line are even more deeply entrenched, aggravating the feeling of deprivation and neglect.

Although all the members of communities are affected by the armed conflict, the impact on women and girls is far greater, because of their status in society and their sex. The region, under the shadow of conflict, has witnessed resurgence of patriarchal values and norms, which have brought with them new restrictions on the movement of women, the dress they wear and more overtly, physical violence such as rape, which is systematically used as a tactic against a particular community. All this is compounded by the long social, economic and psychological trauma.[11]

Apart from conflict which makes both women and girls

extremely vulnerable to violence, there are other reasons for women's vulnerability. Every human being requires certain basics for existence. But even though 66 years have elapsed since India became Independent, and 64 years since Manipur merged with India, Manipur remains a state neglected, where its denizens are deprived of basic amenities such as regular power supply, running water, proper sanitation and drainage, proper road infrastructure; and are also plagued by inflation of prices of essential commodities, caused in part by continuous economic blockades and strikes. Denial of basic rights is a violation of human rights, but the violation impacts women more, as their burden increases—for instance much time and energy has to be expended on collecting water from streams, rivers, ponds, (even the Kangla Moat water is sold in barrels) as only a few areas get a supply of water for a short time on certain days of the week, whereas many areas even in Imphal have no regular water supply, and water has to be bought. Water does not come cheap and women with a limited budget or earning are hard put to save money for buying water, which the government is supposed to supply on a daily basis. The physical labour involved in the hill terrain not only ages women, but gives rise to other health problems like pain in the back and joints, because of the miles they have to trek both downhill and uphill, and also because of the heavy load they have to daily carry. The scarcity of water has been fuelled by the trend in urbanization which has resulted in traditional water bodies-pukhris in every leikai (colony) being filled up and then built upon. Again, L.P.G. is not always available, more so in the remote parts of the state, and in times of economic blockades, its price is so exorbitant, (₹ 2000/- for a cylinder) that women have to have recourse to firewood or charcoal as kitchen fuel. Impoverished women, especially in the hills have again to expend time and labour in collecting the much needed firewood for the kitchen hearth.

The use of power which is taken for granted all over the world as a basic necessity, is so scarce as it be literally 'invisible', despite the hype generated by government hydro electric plants, which supposedly would put an end to both the power crisis and water scarcity, the ground reality is that except for the men in power, the rest of the state receives power for a maximum of 5 to 6 hours in twenty-four hours. And this limited supply is certainly not assured-most of the transformers as also transmission lines are so poorly maintained, that breakdowns are frequent and inevitable. And when a transformer 'bursts' it is anybody's guess, when a new or the repaired transformer will commence functioning, as such actions proceed at a snail's pace. The only alternative is to have recourse to inverters and generators which can be bought at relatively cheap prices as they come to Manipur from countries of South East Asia through Myanmar (Manipur shares an international border with Myanmar). But inverters need to be charged and that is again not a certainty, because of the erratic and poor power supply; generators have to be run on petrol or diesel, both of which products continue to escalate in price. Once again it is marginalized poor women who suffer the most, because they are compelled to use candlelight to cook the evening meal. And some villages have reported using pine torches for purpose of lighting a house. This alternative again takes a toll of women's health and energy-collecting sufficient pine for torches.

With references to sanitation and drainage especially during the monsoons, a glance at the condition of the women's markets and the public thoroughfares, where garbage is indiscriminately littered, would bring to focus, the fact that in earning a livelihood, women have to struggle against great odds, especially women who are carting produce to the markets from distant areas and who have to trek muddy, slippery roads carrying heavy loads to markets which too are anything but hygienic. Despite year round black topping of major arterial roads, one heavy shower renders them practically impassable for women pedestrians, as all the roads are pitted with potholes in which water collects, stagnates and breeds disease. There is always the danger of an accident, besides women's garments became badly stained with dirty muddy marks- the poorer women who cannot afford washing machines, have to expend much labour in ridding their garments of these stains. It also takes a toll on footwear which translates into added expenditure, which could have been avoided if proper facilities existed.

The absence of these also has a bearing on women's health. For instance if inter-district and inter-village roads are mere muddy tracts cut into the steep hillside they become impassable not only during the rains but because of landslides which are frequent. An ailing elderly woman, a young pregnant woman has no option but to walk to the closest PHC (Primary Health Centre) or her male relatives carry her in a bamboo stretcher over ravines and forests, only to find that neither doctor, nurses, medical equipment nor drugs are available at the PHC. They then have to journey farther– usually to the district headquarters or the capital city. Delay in diagnosis or delay in treatment causes the sick to become sometimes critically ill. There are of course ASHA's in the rural areas who assist especially in getting pregnant women to hospitals for institutional deliveries, but all too often even the print media highlights the plight of women who during or after the delivery succumb to death for no ostensible reason. The vulnerability of women especially the marginalized like those infected with HIV is apparent in the treatment meted out to such women especially in government hospitals. No doubt ART medicines are given free of cost to many such women, but those are only available at designated centres, which because of distance or poverty is out of the reach of many women. But discrimination and stigmatism shown to such women makes them fearful of getting treatment at health centres. As far as the vast majority of not only low income women, but also women of the middle strata are concerned, proper treatment is not given at governmental health centres/institutions, because most of the government doctors are working not only in the institution to which they are appointed, and earning a huge salary, but they are working before and after office hours in private hospitals and clinics, which pay rich dividends monetarily. They naturally tend to direct the women to these institutions where they are made to undergo a battery of tests before being treated- these tests cost a tidy sum of money and put a great strain on the family budget. There is the ever present danger of a doctor attending a patient making a mistake out of sheer tiredness-the doctors seem to work all hours; However the irony is that because the government cannot ensure peace and security in the state, if a patient falls critically ill at night, it is near impossible to access a doctor, as they do not venture out at night, except for government doctors, who are on call at the hospital. Timely health interventions at an affordable cost are generally not within the reach of most women.

For these reasons the epithet 'a failed state' has been given to Manipur. 'Manipur has since long became a failed state. Corruption of all kinds has eaten away its foundations. Elected members with little or no vision at all, have been busy making ministry after ministry, but never have the time to run the government. On paper, successive ministries had already undertaken projects after projects, the list is endless' but the reality is that there is no semblance of these projects at the ground level.[12] Not only can the state not ensure that women have access to basic needs, but because they have not created conditions which ensure security and freedom, women's livelihood is also at stake. In a non-industrialised state with predominant agrarian economy where the agricultural land is shrinking because of projects taken up by the state in the name of development (mega dams), and because of rapid urbanization, rural to urban migration, the opportunities for sustainable livelihood are almost non-existent, miring women in poverty especially in the hill areas. Frequent economic blockades which the government is unable to prevent drains women of their hard earned income, thereby increasing their vulnerability. In the protracted blockades of 2011, the government made arrangements for essential goods to be brought by truckers escorted by security personnel. However, the purpose was largely defeated, because there was such an escalation in prices, which again the government failed to check, that many of the goods were out of the reach of the common woman. And it is the woman who is tasked with preparing the meal and feeding the family.

Despite the Right to Education for all children under the age of 14 being implemented in the state, because of lack of both teachers and infrastructure or absence of both, many poor women also prefer to send their children to private schools despite the higher costs, and the fact that a free midday meal is given to children in government educational institutions. The higher costs of education places great stress on women who have to work harder and sacrifice more to educate their children. It also leads to many poor women especially from the interiors of the hills, handing over their children to well run orphanages outside the state where they would receive free education, free board and lodge. Unfortunately, most of these children suffer abuse-instead of being provided with facilities for learning, they are cooped up in small crowded rooms, and their services are used for domestic purposes—cleaning, washing, cooking etc. But these are the more fortunate children, in contrast to those who are sexually abused, and physically intimidated through beatings and other forms of abuse. Only recently 51 such children were rescued from an orphanage in Jaipur, many came back physically deformed—unable to even walk properly. This occurred in the first half of 2013 in March. The trauma of the mothers on learning about the ordeal their children suffered has made the women more fragile and vulnerable.

Vulnerability of women renders it possible for non-state actors to recruit them to serve demand notes on individuals or organizations or to lobby grenades. These women are susceptible to persuasion because they tend to come from the more vulnerable section of society—either they are widows or they suffer from HIV, or are greatly impoverished. A security personnel narrated how one such woman was denied entrance to a facility where she was to serve a demand note (extortion) so she disguised herself in a doctor's garb and gained entry.[13] Recently, the media has highlighted the fact that some women have been used to recruit child soldiers.

The vulnerability of women is also exacerbated by a change in the ethos of Manipur. This is best illustrated by the fact Irom Sharmila's movement now in the thirteenth years remains an individual movement, to be applauded and talked about[14] even though it is perhaps the longest non-violent struggle undertaken by a woman anywhere.(She is detained in the security ward of a government hospital and forcibly nose-fed to keep her alive). The woman in Manipur who was looked upto and revered in the role/ capacity of 'Mother' is no longer a sacrosanct figure, evident from the increasing violations of women's chastity. It would seem that many such crimes have been committed by rogue elements who take advantage of the ongoing conflict, to fish in troubled waters.[15]

And because women symbolize the culture of the land, their bodies often become targets-symbols of victory or defeat. This is especially relevant in feuds over possession of territory/land. Women who have suffered rape are so traumatized that they are driven to commit suicide-well known cases are those of Naobi, Rose and Sangita. In combing operations women are especially vulnerable, even though women try to protect themselves by forming collectives. They live in fear-husbands, sons, and fathers' maybe picked up, detained, tortured or killed or reported missing. One woman narrated an incident that occurred to her as a child. Armed men came to check her house after calling all the male family members outside. The woman then a young girl with cropped hair and dressed in shorts was also suspect believing her to be a boy. This incident left a permanent mark on her psyche.[16] This is not a solitary instance. There is constant frisking and checking of males especially young men all the year round. Women- in the capacity of mothers, wives, sisters, aunts remain fearful, that their relatives will be detained or taken for interrogation, sometimes never to return. Because agriculture is the mainstay of the economy in the hill areas, 'Naga Women's vulnerability has increased because the traditional governance structure headed by the chief who wielded authority has been rendered largely redundant with formation of ADC's (Autonomous District Councils) and what a Naga woman activist termed as government encroachment on their customary land. This deprives women of their moorings. Moreover because of the ongoing movement for a 'Greater Nagaland' the Naga women who may have no part in the movement are viewed with suspicion.[17] Women's collectives which are formed to protect men are also vulnerable because not only the security forces but also the state police look at them in an uncomplimentary manner. Many areas of the state especially those located in the hills have asked for the withdrawal of security forces because they take undue advantage of the power and authority vested in them. Paradoxically, many women are putting money together to get their sons/husbands employed in the army or police—as such a career ensures financial stability— however the rates (illegal) for entry are extremely high amounting to several lacs of rupees. This increases women's vulnerability as they are hard put to find the necessary finance; (Corruption is endemic in other sectors of the government as well) and experience great stress. The anxiety and stress takes a toll of women's health and they become prone to problems like high blood pressure depression, diabetes, stomach and heart ailments. Women usually are the last in a family to get treated for any illness, and their poor mental/physical state prevents them from making the best use of their capabilities.

Most poignant is the plight of a group of women who have been referred to as Widows of the Gun in a Dutch publication.[18] These are young women who for different reasons, sometimes beyond their control, have contracted early marriages to men who have for some reasons been linked to non state actors-the men became suspect and were shot dead in what is known in popular parlance in Manipur as 'fake encounters'. The young widows, all with small children have to mourn not only the loss of a husband, but also contend with the reality that the bread earners of the family are no more, and poverty stares stark into their faces. These widows, find it difficult to eke out an existence, because they themselves are viewed with suspicion on the grounds that they were married to 'supposed terrorists'. Also because of the circumstances surrounding the death of their husbands, these widows cannot procure a death certificate and so are barred from the pension scheme for widows in the state. The pension scheme is itself inadequate for the large numbers of widows in Manipur-the amount given is meager- ₹ 200/- per month. Only 2000 widows are eligible, whereas the recorded number of widows is supposedly over 10,000. And even to get the meager amount the widow has to offer some monetary gratification. Women above the age of forty years only are eligible the logic underpinning this regulation is that women below forty can easily remarry and so do not require a pension. But if a woman's husband is killed by a non state actor, the state awards her a monetary compensation. The plight of conflict widows remains miserable.[19]

One widow expressed herself in the words: My husband was a surrendree, and he had not been related with any underground outfit or activity for the last ten years before he was killed in a reported encounter by security forces. Lata has to cope with the loss of her husband and the burden of raising children. Like Lata, many women have had to confront such a predicament. Lata's husband did not get the benefits provided under the surrender and rehabilitation scheme. (₹ 2000/- per month for 35 months and ₹ 1.5 lakh as bank fixed deposit).[20]

The environment of fear and insecurity, lack of sustainable employment opportunities, disappointment, depravation, leads both impoverished and displaced women as also young women to have recourse to illicit drugs or alcohol. This in turns has a spiraling effect, the vulnerability of such women increases, because women users are looked down upon, and it is not easy for these women to get out of the clutch of illicit drugs, especially as these are easily available because of the porous Indo-Myanmar border and Manipur's proximity to the Golden Triangle. The emergence of nuclear families and the break-up of the traditional joint family which provided support, help, advice, solace in difficulties, has also an impact on women's vulnerability to drugs—in the absence of a caring atmosphere, women yield to pressure and become addicted to drugs or alcohol. There are also women who traffic in drugs-but most such women are petty traders who take up such work primarily to make ends meet. Although trafficking in drugs certainly cannot be condoned, these small women traffickers are harassed much more than the actual kingpins in the narcotic trade-most such women enjoy a low socio-economic status.

Women remain vulnerable because of both under-development as also unemployment. There are links between rampant violence and lack of people oriented development. 'In Manipur there is no development. There is no industry. Everything is being imported; we do not have enough agriculture to feed rice to people round the year. There are no jobs, for any job a huge bribe has to be paid. Rather than development, Manipur is experiencing the 'development of under-development'. No significant employment opportunities have been created. (a limited skill development programme has recently been launched by the state government) Rampant unemployment has lead to widespread frustration and alienation. A scramble ensues for scare opportunities, resources and jobs. At stake is the basic well being of families, clans and communities. Sharmila is questioning the model of profit-led development—the violence the state is experiencing is a part of a pattern of neglect, exploitation and underdevelopment.[21]

The phenomena of under-development coupled with unemployment has compelled many young women to leave the state in search of jobs. (The pull of urbanization also plays its part). Some of these young women are well educated whereas some are drop-outs at the school or college level. However, both categories are equally vulnerable as they are generally naïve about realities of life outside Manipur especially in Metropolitan cities like Delhi, Mumbai, Bangalore, Pune, etc., where they tend to gravitate in search of employment. Because of their innocence and gullibility, they are often duped by potential or actual employers in matters of reimbursement, other facilities which are mandatory on employers. And some of them are unwittingly lured into the sex-trade. There are reports of how the young pretty women are first invited to parties where they are flattered and given much attention. Gradually they are forced into part or full time prostitution against their will. As they have no safety net to fall back upon, it becomes difficult for them to get out of the trap, and they usually lack the finances to return home, where there are no job opportunities available to them. There are other women who work in shopping malls, spas, restaurants, call centres etc. who are equally vulnerable, especially those who work night shifts or return home late at night. Their different or so-called exotic features coupled with the mistaken perception that young women from the North East are promiscuous, leads men to make unwanted attacks on their modesty—some of these have fatal consequences as evinced in the recent death of a Tangkhul young woman from Manipur, at Delhi-May 2013. The young woman's post mortem was conducted twice, but the report was not furnished to her family at home in Manipur, and her dead body was found in suspicious circumstances in the flat she had rented at Delhi—there were tell tale marks on the body which would point to rape or some form of physical assault. Young women from Manipur are extremely vulnerable to sexual harassment when working outside the state, and many such incidents have been highlighted by the local media. In fact a North-East Helpline has been set up at Delhi precisely to help these victims.

With the provision of enhanced connectivity of the Northeast States with other parts of the country, as also the pull factor of the market, women in Manipur have become vulnerable to trafficking. The modus operandi is quite subtle—a native woman especially one living in a less developed part of the state, is recruited by an agent from outside the state, to supply young women for domestic and other allied jobs like beauty parlour assistants, as masseurs etc. (the last is specially popular in Goa where many young tribal women of Manipur work as massage therapists in hotels specially dotted around the beaches). Instead of providing the women with safe jobs which provide a sustainable income, many of the women are trafficked to brothels and they become even more vulnerable especially as their status registers a sharp decline. In recent years police and activists have raised the alarm that human traffickers are increasingly turning to India's poor and insurgency—ridden North-Eastern States in their search for young girls to work in big city brothels. Activists estimate that thousands of North East girls disappear every year—most of whom are not reported by families due to the stigma associated with being part of the sex trade. Due to preoccupation with counter-insurgency operations and high priority for law and order duties, the problem of trafficking has been low in the list of priorities of the police.[22] But according to the IPC Year Wise Statement of Crime Against Women from the year 2006-2011 for the state of Manipur, surprisingly no cases are registered under Immoral Traffic (P) Act except for one case in 2007 and one in 2008[23]. Women targeted for trafficking fall into three categories-single women, women who eloped but returned to their natal home without entering into matrimony, and widows. It would appear that such women are easy bait because of their lower status[24]. But a causative factor is the dearth of suitable employment opportunities for women which does construe a violation of their fundamental rights—this often forces them to work outside the state in a work not of their choice. If the government properly tapped the tourist potential of the state, many such women would find employment in hotels, guest houses, restaurants, which are required by tourists and also as guides and tour operators.

But trafficking of women also exists within the state. A good number of commercial sex workers (CSW's) are rural girls employed in Imphal as also other townships, but there are some women who have joined this profession to earn quick, easy money. A consequence of displacement caused by ethnic clashes was a spurt in trafficking of women (especially tribals). Another section of such women have become CSW's because of economic compulsion—the only means of survival for themselves and their family.

There can be no doubt that with the erosion of the traditional social capital to care for all members of an extended family or local community, women's vulnerability has increased. This is compounded by the fact that no proper support systems are in place for women. And women who earn more than their husbands or whose husbands do not have any earnings experience a different form of vulnerability. 'If we look at the proportion of recruitments in government in recent years, women are fairly well represented, outstripping the men. It is significant that this upward mobility of women is happening at the higher end of the pyramid. Women have joined the ranks of top professionals on an equal footing with their male counterparts. (Evident from the results of the UPSC and MPSC examinations held in recent years.) Women are also definitely set to dominate the profession of teaching. What is more surprising is that Manipur women have broken the glass ceiling, to claim their places even in the traditionally male bastion of the police forces. Two factors have enabled this transformation-education and change in the nature of economy—from manufacturing, agriculture and labour intensive industry to knowledge and service oriented industry. It's a level playing field. Women may start earning more than men, pro-women's policies may be introduced in the workplace, and women holding bigger purse strings will have a greater say in family affairs. Many men will not like the new gender equation'.[25] Obviously there would be a fall out, because men would resent the women's superior status, but would be content to be supported financially—this in turn would cause discontent or unhappiness in the women, who finds the man trying to dominate the public space, and not giving her sufficient freedom to express her own views. Such husbands tend to dominate in other ways too—for e.g. A salaried professional women who takes a bank loan to build a house, is not permitted by her husband to put the property in her own name, but she continues to pay the principal and interest on the loan. As a result her position is precarious; it would be more so on the death of a husband, as adult children or other relatives may turn her out of the house, which she has no legal claim to, as the *patta* is in her husband's or some other male relatives name.

The erosion of social capital has been accompanied by a decline in ethics and moral values. This leads to an upsurge in crime against women. For instance the recent (June 2013) Video clip of a nude couple making love filmed by IRB (Indian Reserve Battalion) personnel who uploaded it on the Net. This act enraged women activists who charged the police station in Churachandpur demanding punishment to the culprits—in the melee that ensued, some women were injured. Two technological inventions have speeded the decline in moral values—The Net and Mobile Phone. Pornographic and other inappropriate contents have lead to a spurt in crimes against women; the perpetuators having lost their moral anchoring they do not feel that they have done anything wrong. Also because of demands of time on working parents, the parents do not instruct children in right values, right thinking, they turn a blind eye to their children's transgressions dismissing them as childish demeanour. When these children grow up they lack a sense of ethics and commit crimes with impunity. The forces of consumerism and globalization also contribute to this phenomena-for instance working women are vulnerable because they are often compelled to give in to the demands of their children for expensive accessories like the latest electronic gadgets, automobiles, expensive flats, while they continue to labour at home and outside to provide for the never ending demand of their children for materials goods.

Many enterprising women, young and middle aged are engaged in border trade (Indo-Myanmar) for their livelihood. These women traders form the majority of the day to day traders who make periodic and hectic journeys from their villages to the trading town at most weekly. However, there is a constant stream and counter stream of exit and entry into border trade. This is indicative of the many risks and uncertainties that surround the profession of women border traders. Some 57.06 per cent women have been in trade for four years. However, 25 per cent have been in trade for over five years.[26]

Conditions in the border town are not conducive to the safety and convenience of women traders and their goods. As a result, they have a few short hours in which to stock their goods (all vehicles departing from Moreh back to Imphal or other towns have to leave not later than 2 P.M. Most of the buses or shared Taxis used for transport leave not earlier than 5 A.M. from Imphal and take about four hours to reach Moreh.) The establishments that cater to traders at Moreh lack basic amenities like power and water supply. (Moreh has much higher temperature than the rest of the state), as also proper toilet facilities. This absence intimidates the women traders, who prefer to return home before nightfall. However, the women face innumerable inconveniences on the return journey—firstly as they are generally petty traders they commute in crowded, poorly maintained taxis that ply the route, and secondly, they are subject to intimidation and harassment on the way. Multiple and time consuming security checks was identified as the biggest problem facing the women traders, 41 per cent of the traders ranked security checks as their biggest problem. Multiple tax collections by state and non state agencies was ranked as the biggest problem to 28 per cent, and bad roads for 24.19 per cent[27]. Light vehicles travelling from Imphal to Moreh are checked nine times starting from Pallel, and the number of checkings is doubled on the return journey, and checking often means payment of money by transporters. On the return journey from Moreh to Imphal, Moreh Customs charge money based on the types and quantity of goods loaded on the vehicles. At Moreh, Hill Tribal Council charges ₹ 30/- on each vehicle, police charge ₹ 20/-, Wireless ₹ 20/-, CID ₹ 20/- ACODOM ₹ 10/- and an unidentified body ₹ 50/-. Vehicles are checked thoroughly at Khudengthabi check post and Tengnoupal check post of Assam Rifles but no money is charged.[28] However the jawans carelessly and indiscriminately delve into women's handbags, and throw their goods on to the road for checking—this results in damage—they also try to intimidate women by their manner of checking.

Tengnoupal police charge ₹ 20/- per vehicle and extra money for goods, Wireless and C I D charge ₹ 25/- each, and an unidentified body opposite to Tengnoupal police collects. ₹ 100/-. The transporters have to pay the same amounts to the same agencies based at Pallel. At Heikakpokpi, Manipur Rifles charges ₹ 20/- and vehicles are charged ₹ 10 to ₹ 20/- by Khongjom Police, ₹ 10/- at Wangjing Police outpost, ₹ 10/- to ₹ 20/- by VDF at Canchipur and ₹ 10/- to ₹ 20/- at Sinajamei Chingamathak.[29] With the incidence of various forms of taxation, the women traders are certainly oppressed—but because they need to earn a livelihood, they persist for some years at least, but their vulnerability remains stark.

Another obvious cause for women's vulnerability is the ethnic clashes that have occurred in the state, mainly because of the assertion of ethnic nationalism. It is recorded that the last decade of the twentieth century in the annals of Manipur will always be remembered for the devastating ethnic clashes in which about

2000 people were killed, 500 villages attacked, 7000 houses destroyed and 1,50,000 displaced[30]. In this context, Tingneichong writes: During the early 1990's, on account of the so-called ethnic cleansing of the NSCN—IM (National Social Council of Nagaland—IssacMuivah), many Kuki women were widowed and made homeless, some were compelled to sustain themselves by recourse to prostitution.[31] To what did these ethnic clashes which increased women's vulnerability have their roots in? There are some common problems which are unique to the entire hill people, and these are enough to generate discontent. The salient problems may be identified as:

1. Geographical isolation and cultural Alienation
2. Problem of a subsistence Economy
3. Problems of exploitation by others
4. Feeling of being ousted by other cultural groups
5. Problems of lop-sided development measures and maladjustment[32]

The ethnic women of the North-East suffers the imposition of the ethnic males regarding preservation of traditional customs and costumes during ethnic movements, mostly without a decision of their own. She is only a giver, because in the patriarchal game of power, she has nothing to gain. On the other hand, during army operations by the Indian State, she is a silent spectator, as her beautiful kept hearth and home is ransacked, her brother and sons killed in the encounter in front of her eyes, and she is finally abused and raped. Neither the Indian State nor insurgency, can safeguard the life and rights of a woman, because she is the common sight/site for both, for enacting the drama of power and violence. From her position of a twice marginalized subject, what is her plausible alternative? Can she go on bearing the violence? Should she articulate a new language of her own, which can redefine her identity as a woman rooted in her culture, outside the violent drama of the state and insurgency. It is interesting to see how a woman of the North-East asserts a female subject hood through her indirect rejection of the logic of the state and insurgency[33].

Most ethnic communities are guided by a patriarchal ideology which looks askance at the growing movement of women for the full enjoyment of rights guaranteed to them under the constitution. Earlier isolated from the larger Indian polity, (till Indian's Independence) it is only recently that ethnic communities have been exposed to a new world view (the advent of colonial rule as also of Christian missionaries did uplift the tribal from the old world to the new). In the process of adjustment and transition the aspirations of one community conflict with the other, as aspirations of the one can only be realised at the expense of the other (for e.g. The Naga demand for Greater Nagaland and Kuki demand for Zalengam—territory contested is common to both). This is exacerbated by the 'Divide and rule' policy of the government—pitting one community against the other—this policy has eroded the common bonding of women of all communities—mistrust erupts into violence. Activities common to all women such as jointly husking rice, caring for children irrespective of which community they belong to, community singing and dancing etc. are now carried out by women of each community separately.[34] There are occasions however when women of all communities come together on a common platform to air their grievances or to fight for justice. 'The conflict is manmade—Manipur is passing through a critical period. The polity is in some sort of a bind or turmoil, actuated by 'some' in the name of a 'struggle'. The freedom of people to speak out has been muffed. The presence of various insurgent outfits has proliferated the complex situation in different layers[35]

What is contested in North-East India is both the forging of post-colonial nationalism by selective appropriation of cultural resources of native communities, and the Indian state that administers such an appropriation, and encodes it as development and democracy for North-East India. But the contest centres itself around the visible dominance of the State, created through socially rooted dominance of certain communities, which has led ethnic communities to struggle both against the state and those dominant communities on whose behalf the state supposedly acts against the interest of the native communities.[36] Moreover, the telos of insurgent outfits is to gain or restore their politics of self preservation and homeostasis, ensuring primarily the communitarian rights of people within the specific ethnic group, the telos of counter insurgent forces is to bring the violent and rebel groups back to a national mainstream, which for the retention of its multi-cultarist perspective, tends to diffuse the cultural specificities of these ethnic groups.[37]

Another cause for women's vulnerability especially among the tribals is that communication in the region is hazardous and acts as a handicap towards economic development of the area. The migration of outsiders and foreigners (Mayangs—non-Manipuris, and Myanmarese/Bangladeshis) complicated land—related ethnic employment problems. The phenomenon of ethnic eruption broadly explains the insurgency in the North-East region. It has been further aggravated by lack of development, total neglect by those in power, exploitation of resources for the benefit of others, lack of opportunities for youth, gross injustice and inequality, widespread social pollution caused by rampant corruption in all spheres of administration, and above all, a deep feeling of alienation among tribal youth.[38] A Naga women was of the view that it is land related problems that cause ethnic conflicts—this has been proved in recent times in feuds occurring between neighbouring villages where residents are of a different community, as for example Silent village in the hill areas and its neighbouring village.

The greatest impact of ethnic clashes on women has been displacement. But while inter tribal violence inflicts high casualties; it is sporadic and restricted geographically to those populations in actual conflict with each other. Since neither the state nor any other authority takes responsibility for the victims, there is little aid for rehabilitation, or effective long term trauma support[39]. Women suffer disproportionately: 'Mental health of women is poor as compared to men. Their mental problems are disproportionally high and only a fraction of women access treatment'.[40] The breakdown of formal health care service due to ethnic conflict exacerbates the problem. Women especially in the hill areas have to travel/trek several kilometres to meet their health needs, and all are not in a position to do so. The result is increase in vulnerability because of poor mental and physical health.

But displacement disrupts the centrality of women's role in family, community and society, generating insecurity and vulnerability. Displacement also disrupts crucial social and cultural linkages, and in resettlement, bonds and networks of trust are replaced by animosity and mistrust.[41] Moreover relief camps and makeshift homes are so basic as to lack amenities such as proper toilets, drinking water, subsidised food grains etc. Moreover women especially are deprived of privacy—their homes are cramped, unhealthy and over-crowded. But women who have been particularly close to nature, whose livelihood is dependent on land (for sustainable cultivation), find themselves suddenly cast adrift with no moorings. Moreover, they lack the training and skill to work in alternative livelihood options—they are reduced to penury, stress and trauma, and driven to seek relief, sometimes in illicit drug use, which however is habit—forming, a drain on their scarce resources, with adverse impact on health and ability to work. They also become vulnerable to HIV through shared injection drug use. Other displaced women who are unable to find employment have recourse to prostitution where again they become vulnerable to both STD's and HIV as they are not in a position to negotiate safe sex practice (Manipur has an extremely high sero-prevalence—27%). Women infected with HIV/AIDS are stigmatised, even their children suffer discrimination, more so, as many of them too are infected. The more marginalised women find it difficult to access both nutritious food supplements as also ART (anti retroviral), because they are unable to go to designated government ART centers, and also do not have the financial means to access nutritional food supplements.

The burden of providing even the essentials for daily living for the family, force displaced women to walk miles to collect a meagre supply of water, firewood, and food provisions like wild herbs, vegetables, fruits, berries etc. It lengthens a women's working hours, Unemployment even of educated youth is high in Manipur. However, employment is generally associated with greasing palms of those in power. A Manipuri Padmashri in a memorial lecture reproduced in a local daily stated: Even if the likes of Anna Hazare undertake *satyagraha* and the country legislates the strongest law to fight corruption, I don't believe corruption can be wiped out, especially from the soil of Manipur. It is precisely because in our society, corruption has been accepted as a fact of life. The virus known as corruption was not imported from the outside. Practice of 'Haijachatpa' (seeking favour) in any activity, which was sanctioned by the prevailing culture of feudalism in Manipur, has taken firm roots in our society.[42] Women find it almost impossible to eradicate corruption as it is so engrained in the culture of the state; they, especially the poorer women, usually lack the financial means to buy a job either for themselves or a family member. The prevalent rates for a female nursing job in a government institute is way beyond their means.

Again, ethnic violence against indigenous and tribal women by police and armed forces is unabated and subject to intermittent extreme outbreaks of mass incidence, which are not apparently reducing, given the apathy of law-makers, justice systems and executive[43].

Ethnic rivalries and nationalism have emerged from an identity crisis-one's place in the larger Indian polity, where there is a danger to ethnic identity through the process of mainstreaming. Ethnic groups have recourse to garnering votes by playing the ethnic card, resulting in a disturbing picture of 'We' and 'they'. The latter will erode their identity. This self consciousness and ethno-nationalism dehumanizes both parties and results in VAW. This is especially relevant to women who marry outside their own communities. Viewing through an ethnic lens prevents a holistic world-view and as the state provides few opportunities to ethnic underprivileged people especially women to excel, ethnic aspirations are articulated within narrow confines. As a government employee phrased it—people at large display a 'crab mentality'—in that if an individual or community is progressing it arouses the ire and jealousy of others, who lose no time in reducing the progress of the other. As the walls of each community grows higher, women become even more vulnerable because opportunities for personal growth, development and employment, become extremely restricted[44].

As groups confront threats to survival, self-esteem and identity, they become defensive. Rigid identity politics is a result of this crisis. Ethnic rivalries have sharpened in Manipur during the past decades, to the point of violent conflagrations. Contemporary ethnic conflicts are symptomatic of a growing sense of vulnerability and insecurity: the polarization of ethnic groups is in fact a recent phenomenon. The current epidemic of violence is associated with the rise of a certain notion of modernity and associated erosion of social customs that encouraged communities to live in harmony. Communities and relations between communities, are being reformulated in the light of contemporary economic and political forces. Leadership of each ethnic group has marshalled distinct sets of 'facts' based on widely divergent versions of history, in which the 'other' is projected as exploiter and perpetrator of violence. As identity politics gains ground, perceptions have sharpened. Peaceful methods of interaction are getting vitiated.[45]

Women in Manipur like all women in South Asia are caught between the demands of a globalising world on the one hand and traditional values and cultural practices on the other. Although active in the economy, they tend to find themselves confined to lower positions with longer hours of work, lower wages, poor working conditions and little job security. The worst affected women are those in the informal sector, where a majority are located, especially the home-based women workers. Entry into the globalising world has also been associated with rising prices, loss of job security, lack of information, social security and health care.[46]

Women also find the centrality of their lives impacted by changes in environment and climate. In Loktak (a large fresh water lake close to Imphal), a woman's work burden has increased, as a result of the decreasing resource base of the common property. For the woman, the necessity to expend more labour and time in fishing and thereafter selling the catch, which is significantly lower to what it was before the resource base of the common property decreased, results in a greater work load, a longer working day especially as her fishing activities do not relieve her of the household chores. Her husband or male relatives too may be fisherman, but their work load is lighter, as they confine their work only to fishing. The fisherwoman is also responsible to cater to the needs of children and other family members. This is why in the protest against the construction of the Tipaimukh Dam in Manipur; a woman is heading the protest, because the construction would adversely impact the environment which provides sustenance to the indigenous population. The mega-dam would deprive women of their livelihood, as also access to forest products, as the construction would involve felling of 7.8 million trees and 27,000 bamboo grooves.[47] The burden of social cost inflicted by such projects often fall on the poor and disadvantaged sections (like women).[48] In the event of the dam getting constructed, the local population would face displacement. Displacement causes serious economic, social and cultural disruptions of the life of the tribal people affected by it. Dispossessed farmers (despite cash compensation) can become landless forever. In Tipaimukh area there are mostly small marginal farmers and food gatherers. Loss of shelter (temporary), joblessness and maginalisation may take place due to shifting of the farm in the resettlement area. Productivity of land may change (e.g. fertility) above all, the 'tightly knit social system in a village (based on mutual co-operation and co-dependence) will be disturbed. The most vulnerable are women, children and the aged—they would be rendered strangers, powerless and marginalised in their new setting. They have to start afresh'. If displaced women especially opt to shift to urban centres, 'they would be reduced to nothing more than slum dwellers because of the high cost of living and their lack of adequate skills'[49].

Women cultivators fear being divorced from land which provides sustenance. It is an intrinsic part of every individual's nature to ownorpossess or to be linked to land in one way or the other. The submergence of land by the hydro project (proposed at Tipaimukh Dam) will enhance the pressure on the surrounding areas by shortening the jhum cycle, (slash and burn method of cultivation practised by the Kukis in particular) affecting environment and the livelihood of jhum dependent communities[50]. Because, the one fundamental fact which distinguishes the indigenous people (tribals of Manipur) from other people, is their emotional attachment to the land where they lived. The land contains their history and sense of identity and it ensures their economic viability as independent people.[51]

Another cause of anxiety to women especially non indigenous women is home or office visits by individuals, groups, organisation demanding money. Some of the demands are for a good cause, but the large majority are a form of extortion, as both individuals and groups take advantage of the absence of law and order to intimidate women and collect money. The attitude of such people is threatening it is not possible to check the credentials of those demanding money, and from fear and insecurity, women are forced to shell out part of their hard earned money, especially if they are alone at home on in the work place. Although most such demands are made by men, there is also some representation of women who in the name of an orphanage or another such worthy cause demand money. But the worthy causes only exist on paper in most cases.

The practice of 'chenba' or elopement also contributes to young women's vulnerability, especially, when a couple who fear that they will not be able to get consent from parents to enter into matrimony, they elope, and live together in a relative or friend's house till the parents give their consent. There are other reasons too for elopement. Usually the woman eloping is young - often naive and immature and not ready to don the mantle of responsibility and duty associated with married women, as she has received no pre-marital counseling- many young women have not completed either their schooling or their higher education, they therefore lack skills for employment in the event of the husband being unable to support the family financially, or in the event of a breakup of the marriage, or disease or early demise of the husband. Also many such young women are not in the know how about family planning, especially the spacing of children, and in the early years of marriage they give birth to two or more children. The upbringing of children is the mother's responsibility and many young mothers find both their mobility and recreational space curtailed, many have no social life as they cannot take small babies or young children with them whenever they leave the house, and many are not in a position to hire a reliable care provider to look after the children in their absence. Professional child minders are in any case not available. Young mothers, especially whose peers are still studying or are working and enjoy considerable independence, envy their friends who are leading such a care-free existence, not bogged down by child care and household responsibilities. Some became envious of their husbands whose social activities are in no way curtailed by marriage or birth of children. The husband's independence and the wife's loss of the same, often creates an atmosphere of stress, tension and mistrust, leading to misunderstandings and even incidents of domestic violence.

Raped women suffer from acute vulnerability. Women re-experience the trauma in memories and dreams, avoiding anything reminiscent of the event, suffer from memory loss, anxiety and severe depression, unable to lead a normal life. Even society (as a whole) hardly offers its sympathies to victims. Rape victims are almost outcast from society and find it almost impossible to marry. The victim has to bear the attached 'shame' as well as the burden of silently coping with the post trauma stress without any or little support. This is because any kind of sexual violence is looked upon by the society as an act of 'dishonour', rather than as a violation of the fundamental human right for every woman.[52] Rape is becoming increasingly common in Manipur.

Again widowhood, changes a woman's life irrevocably. A widow has not only to mourn the loss of a husband, but all too often mourn also the source of livelihood provided by him. Widowhood affects identity, physical safety mobility, access to basic goods and services necessary for survival, rights to inheritance, land and property. Women whose husband have 'disappeared' or are 'missing' experience similar problems as widows do, but without official recognition of their status. They suffer the psychological effects and insecurity that stems from not knowing their husband's fate, and not being able to bury their loved ones and mourn properly, the long term consequences of raising children without a father and not being able to marry. The situation can become desperate for those who have to assume responsibility for dependent family members. Furthermore social traditions may be abandoned by families so overburdened by economic hardship that they can no longer cope, or by families that no longer see themselves as being under any obligation towards the widow. If the link between the family and the woman has been severed by the death of the man, the widow may not always be allowed to keep his children.[53] Even well educated working widows are forced out of their marital house especially when they are barren—they are stigmatised and made to feel redundant. They are deprived even of insurance and health policies where the deceased husband has named them as beneficiaries.

Divorcees are not looked down upon as such in Manipur. Rarely are legal divorces had recourse to-separation is more common. Either way, the single woman can continue her life, but she is usually burdened by having to provide single-handedly for her children, as either she doesn't have the inclination or the knowledge to petition the court for alimony, or is intimidated by the court procedure, inability to find an honest lawyer, or the expenses involved. When she returns to her natal house, she also has to take care of the extended family especially aged parents or relatives, and she usually suffers from financial insecurity.

Widows and divorcees were allowed to remarry or lead a life of their own, For instance, Angoupampa Kyamba the King of Angom took King Lamkyamba's widow (1512-1523. AD) Queen Changning Phabi—mother of Nongyinphaba as wife. But this does not mean that society treated them equally as other women, men who married them, as also their offspring, were banned from attending certain religious rites and rituals such as Lai Haraoba, inheriting Pibapham[54].

Women's vulnerability has increased because as a bureaucrat puts it—'governance shows in fact few signs of actual governance'. It is the primary duty of the state to ensure conditions of peace and security, but instead it fails to prevent endemic bandh and blockades which cover approximately one-third of every year, literally, resulting in 'snatching the morsels of food out of the mouths' of daily wage labourers and vendors (the majority of women are vendors and women lalourers are commonly employed at construction sites to carry the construction materials or clean the sand, stones etc.). Loss of such a large substantial income deprives women dependent on daily earnings, to provide the basic necessities of the family, especially education and health care. Young girls, who are forced out of school because of the mother's inability to pay the school fees, become vulnerable to trafficking.[55] In a similar vein a local daily. The Imphal Free Press, had reported correctly in an editorial: One of the factors that is throwing the state into total atrophy is the fact that increasingly the idea of violence as a language is being given legitimacy precisely by lack of credible and effective governance. There is general failure to recognize the systematic nature of women's subordination. There is a tendency to view abuse and violation of women's human rights as individual aberrations rather than as gender-based violence. The reluctance to characterize the subordination of women as human rights violation is a result of deep rooted, cultural, traditional and age old practices. Even the state, which is generally ready to regulate and intrude into most areas of civil life especially with regard to freedom of expression, is singularly averse to interfering in the private areas of family.[56]

Another factor that impacts women's vulnerability is the 'double standards' of morality applicable to women and men. History records that Maharaja Garibniwaz forcibly took Thambalnu—(a pregnant married women.) after killing her husband. So also, a King of Moirang presented his pregnant wife Ngangkhaleima to his Nobleman Puremba as a token of gratitude for saving his life.[57] It is impossible to imagine a scenario where a woman can forcibly take away another's husband or gift her own husband to another woman. A young woman journalist phrases it—'as per the so called patriarchal rules, every man has the privilege of 'Khongbaan-Chonglaga-kokpa'—excuses, no matter the number of times he is caught indulging in any type of immoral deed or perverted act. However, there is no excuse for the fair sex. She bears, and is regularly compelled to face, the brunt of 'Minokmichie' in the society, if she is ever found in locally defined uncompromising positions and situations. When a married guy indulges in an extra marital affair, it is termed as 'ngaosinaba,' for a married woman it is instead 'lamchatnaidabi' and 'oktabi'.[58] The Punishment for a woman's infidelity can amount to depriving her almost of the right to live—by inflicting third degree burns, so that the woman's life hangs in the balance. Even if she recovers she cannot live a normal existence—she is shunned by all. There are other instances of severe or fatal physical abuse inflicted on such women, sometimes merely on grounds of suspicion.

Even in the earlier historical period, during colonial rule, the control of the market, (where women dominated) or trade and commerce, slipped away from the hands of women. "Our trade and commerce is in the hands of women, but when the goods reached the amount of a maund, they seem to lose confidence', (because of being uneducated)[59]. In the August edition of Yakairol 1931, Randhoni Devi, a teacher of Balika school wrote: 'there remains no pleasure for women in trade as well as domestic life- no one appreciates women in spite of they working selflessly for the family. In the field of trade and commerce, they could not match the shrewd outside traders (non Manipuris-primarily Marwaris). Women were disgraced in the market place, in the name of religion. They had to bear polygamy, as well as wife-beating, they were also blamed for any transgression.[60]

When the Marbak Jagoi Sabi (Commercial dancers) gave performances outside Manipur during Durga Puja, and also entertained the armies during World War II[61] (in Manipur) their vulnerability was exposed- in that the entertainment they provided had the effect of lowering their status in society.[62]

Although today Manipur can boast of crossing even the 33 per cent reservation in electing women leaders in the level of local self-government, these representations of women in Panchayat, Zilla Parishad etc. has not cut much ice, as the women representatives cannot come out of the corrupt political culture, thus diminishing their effectiveness in these institutions. They have also not been able to break the patriarchal hegemonizing ideology which encompasses the state machinery as well as the family.[63] The reservation of the offices of the pradhan and up-pradhan for women has ensured their participation in the affairs of the village. But the husbands are often seen trying to influence their wife members-taking over from them even in official meetings.[64]

Women also feel bound by the Chatnabi, the rigid social norms, the customary laws and traditions. They fear adverse consequences if they do not abide by these societal norms. For instance, a Meitei bride has to allow her groom to eat first from the wedding plate of food served to them-after he has partaken of his fill, she eats what is left from the same plate. This custom could be a charming symbol of togetherness, but at the same time why is it that the woman has to eat last? This practice is continued in their married life—not that the wife eats from the same plate, but she serves the husband first, and then only partakes of the meal. Some affluent husbands are accustomed to going out in the evenings for the purpose of meeting friends. They return late home, and the wife is expected to wait on the husband and serve his food hot, and then clear up after him—in essence—she is the last to retire for the night. Customary law prevents tribal women from having a voice in village councils, administration. Even in church related affairs, women are put in charge of singing in the choir, or preparing and serving the meal, but only a few have some say in decision making, even though all churches have women's associations.

There are certainly some exceptions—two enterprising Manipur women viz. YumnamIbetombi Devi and OinamIbetombi Devi both hailing from Bishenpur district, had been conferred the First National Innovators Award by the President of India at the 7th National Grassroots Technological Innovations and

Traditional Knowledge Awards event at New Delhi for developing a herbal based medicine to cure' coccidiosis'—a disease affecting poultry. But there vulnerability lies in their lack of capital for setting up a manufacturing unit, compounded by the 'lackadaisical attitude and lack of initiative of the state government'.[65] Other successful women entrepreneurs in the field of business are vulnerable to extortion by individuals, organizations, legal and otherwise, as also rogue elements who proliferate in the disturbed conditions of the state.

Although several welfare schemes for the betterment and empowerment of women have been introduced by both the central and the state government, in the word of a woman activist: "these schemes are not need based especially in the context of women at the grass root level—they are more akin to doles, and doles do not serve the purpose of empowering them.[66] Although substantial sums of money are sanctioned, little of these funds actually trickle down to the beneficiaries. And some women beneficiaries are hampered in garnering benefits of projects like the MNREGS-for instance a woman engaged under this scheme is often carrying a baby on her back, because neither a crèche nor provision for caring for young children is provided. Again many vocational trainings imparted to women e.g. Making detergents, soaps, jams, pickles, candied fruits/berries do not enable them to earn a sustainable livelihood, because these products cannot compete with the standardised, well-packaged products of multi-national companies, which are often cheaper than home-made products. Vocational training has to be tailored towards ensuing both food and financial security for women.

Another woman activist states that a lot of money is sanctioned by the centre for development in Manipur. But this money is misused primarily because of a nexus that exists between those in power-both state and non state and contractors. In a recent inspection of 80 Anganwadi Centres just surveyed only 25 per cent were functioning. Workers and helpers-usually mainly women, have not been paid for 14 months despite the fact that 90 per cent of the honorarium to be paid to them is borne by the centre. Where is the money released by the centre to meet the payment of the workers and helpers gone? At best, one may expect official statements, which hide and confuse people more, rather than throw any light on the matter.[67] This is an illustration of how government sponsored schemes work. However the Social Welfare Minister A.K. Mirabai clarified immediately after the inspection that 14 months honorarium cannot be paid, 5 months would be paid as the centre had released the first installment of ₹ 14,81,83,000/- for the first three months of 2013-2014. Moreover the Principal Secretary Social Welfare is stationed at Delhi to lobby the Union Government to release backlog shares.[68] But this promise to pay pending honorarium came only after the matter was made public about the plight of anganwadi workers. However the Secretary of All Manipur ICDS Employee's Union, S. Nirvarani said non payment of salary to over 700 employees of the department for a year, had been creating serious problems to the employees. She added that ₹ 14.81 crore released by the Ministry of Women and Child Development in the first phase and second installment ₹ 11.85 crores are too meagre, as the combined amount would be hardly able to clear about 4 months salaries. She questioned the inability of the Government of Manipur to ensure regular salary to its employees, when neighbouring states like Assam, Mizoram and Nagaland have no such problems.[69] How can women deprived of their hard earned salary for more than a year, sustain themselves and their families—their fundamental rights to livelihood are being violated. And these women are government employees. How much more difficult it is for women in the unorganized sector to earn a livelihood, when government cannot pay women in service, do they have the time or inclination to improve the livelihood of women not in service? Something not talked about but widely prevalent is the extortion, large or small indulged in by the state police forces.[70] This is illustrated in the police allowing unlicensed woman vendors to ply their trade on public thoroughfares on the payment of a certain gratification.

It is quite evident that despite the respect and honour accorded to women—a good illustration would be the accolades given to

Table 3.1: State-wise, Category-wise and Year-wise Statement (Compiled) Showing Opening Balance, Institution, Disposal and Pendency in the Sub-Ordinate Courts of District & Sessions Division, Manipur West

		2009				*2010*				*2011 (upto the 30th Sept. 2011)*			
Sl. No.	*Category of Case*	*Opening Balance*	*Insti-tution*	*Dis-posal*	*Pandency at the end of the year*	*Opening Balance*	*Insti-tution*	*Dis-posal*	*Pendancy at the end of the year*	*Opening Balance*	*Insti-tution*	*Dis-posal*	*Pendancy at the end of the year*
1.	Session Case: Type 1	29	3	6	26	26	22	5	42	42	5	4	43
2.	Session Case: Type 2	24	18	4	38	38	2	27	13	13	1	9	5
3.	Criminal Appeals	1	8	5	4	4	6	5	5	5	4	3	6
4.	Criminal Revision	9	4	11	2	2	13	8	7	7	7	4	10
5.	Warrant procedure PC	404	77	104	377	377	129	163	343	343	80	93	*324
6.	Summons Procedures	34	42	42	34	34	41	38	37	37	167	170	34
7.	Food Adulteration												
8.	NDPS Act Cases	34	43	26	51	51	7	4	54	54	10	21	43
9.	Cases Under Electricity Act	X	X	X	X	X	X	X	X	X	X	X	6
10.	Essential Commodity Act												
11.	Cases Under 123 Cr.P.C												
12.	Case under Domestic Violence Act	8	17	11	14	14	2	X	15	16	28	11	*32
13.	N.I Act Cases												
14.	M.V. Act Cases												
15.	Excise Act Cases												
16.	Juvenile Act Cases												
17.	Forest Act Cases												
18.	Wild Life Cases												
19.	Cinematography/Copy right Act Cases												
20.	Other Criminal Cases not covered above	415	2899	2885	429	429	2745	2717	457	457	2603	2288	*756
Sub-Total (A)		**958**	**3111**	**3094**	**975**	**975**	**2967**	**2968**	**974**	**974**	**2911**	**2508**	***1259**

Table 3.2: Statement Showing Opening Balance, Institution and Pendency of Cases Under Domestic Violence Act in the Courts Under the Judgeship of District and Sessions Judge, Manipur West [4th Quarterly Ending December 2011 (01-10-2011 to 31-12-2011)]

Sl. No	*Court of*	*Opening Balance*	*Institution during the quarter*	*Disposal during the quarter*	*Pendency of cases at the end of the quarter*	*Remarks*
1.	All the Courts under the Judgeship of District and Session Judge, M/W	32	15	7	35	5 cases transferred

Table 3.3: Information Regarding the Total Number of Applications and Appeals filed, Case Disposed of and Number of both Interim and final, Passed by the Courts during the Period from 1st April, 2011 to 31st December, 2011 in the Court (The Judgeship of District and Sessions Division, Manipur West)

Name of Courts	*Information for the period from the 1st April, 2011 to the 31st December, 2011*						
	Total No. of Applications/Appeals filed from 01-04-2011 to 31-12-2011			*Cases disposed of from 01-04-2011 to 31-12-2011*	*No. of Orders passed in the period between 01-04-2011 to 31-12-2011*		
	No. of Applications	*No. of Appeals*	*Total*		*No. of Interim Orders*	*No. of Final Orders*	*Total*
Session Judge, Manipur West	X	2	2	2	X	2	2
Additional Session Judge M/W	X	X	X	X	X	X	X
Additional Session Judge (FTC), M/W	X	X	X	X	X	X	X
Chief Judicial Magistrates of Sessions Division, Manipur West.	24	X	24	23	1	9	10
Judicial Magistrate First Class of Sessions Division, Manipur West.	19	X	19	4	2	4	6
TOTAL	**43**	**2**	**45**	**29**	**3**	**15**	**18**

(K. Bipinchandra Sharma)
District and Session Judge,
Manipur West

Table 3.4: Order Passed by Magestrial and Appelate Courts Under the Protection of Women from Domestic Violence Act, 2010 (For the Period from 1st April, 2010 to 31st December, 2010)

Number of Orders passed by Magisterial Courts		*Number of Order passed by Appellate Courts*		*Total number of Orders passed by both Magisterial and Appellate Courts.*
Name of Magisterial Courts	*Number of Orders passed*	*Name of Appellate Courts*	*Number of Order Passed*	
Chief Judicial Magistrate	98	1. Session Judge	5	
Addl. Chief Judicial. Magistrate	X	2. Addl. Sess. Judge	X	
Divisional Judicial Magistrate	X	3. Addl. Sess. Judge (FTC)	X	
Magistrate 1st Class	72			
Magistrate 2nd Class	X	.		
Total	**170**		**5**	**176**

Table 3.5: Orders Passed by Magistrial and Appellate Courts under the Protection of Women from Domestic Violence Act, 200 (For the Period from 1st January, 2011 to 31st March, 2011)

Number of Orders Passed by Magisterial Courts		*Number of Order Passed by Appellate Courts*		*Total Number of Orders Passed by both Magisterial and Appellate Courts.*
Name of Magisterial Courts	*Number of Orders Passed*	*Name of Appellate Courts*	*Number of Order Passed*	
Chief Judicial Magistrate	15	1. Session Judge	5	
Addl. Chief Judl. Magistrate	X	2. Addl. Sess. Judge	X	
Divisional Judl. Magistrate	X	3. Addl. Sess. Judge (FTC)	X	
Magistrate 1st Class	6			
Magistrate 2nd Class	X			
Total	**22**		**X**	**22**

Mary Kom; women as a whole are vulnerable in many different ways, and this vulnerability renders them easy targets for violence. It doesn't matter whether a woman is rich or poor, educated or illiterate, old or young; all women suffer from fear and insecurity in a large or small measure.

References

1. Salam Irene, Manipur: Land, People, Demography, p. 62, Madhu Rajput, Editor, *Understanding North East India*.
2. Manipur: A Memorandum on Extrajudicial, Arbitrary or Summary Executions submitted by Civil Society Coalition on Human Rights in Manipur and the UN, March 2012, p. 2.
3. *Ibid., op. cit.*
4. Babloo Loitangbam, APSPA turns 55 years: Key Note Address, March 2012.
5. Gaikhamsin Riamei, Violation of Human Rights in North East India, p. 11.
6. Venetia Salesm *op. cit.* pp. 9-10 cit. Surjit Sen Gupta, Conflict and Society: A Sociological Analysis, p. 72, *Journal of NEICSSR*, Vol. 35.
7. Swati Thakur. Insurgency Aftermanth Devestation for Women, p. 502, cit. Patricia Mukhim: Women and Insurgency, The Telegraph No. 29, 2005 cit in Madhu Rajput ed., *Social and Cultural Stratification in North East India*.
8. Anuj Kanchan Datta Roy, Human Rights, Women and Conflict Situations. The Scenario in North East India cit. Elizabeth Imti 2009: Domestic Violence and Guns, www.morung express.com.
9. Ranjana Mishra (2002), Gender Equality and Status of Manipuri Women p. 545 cit. in Madhu Rajput, Editor, *op. cit.*, Support Services to Counter Violence Against Women in Assam, A Resource Directory, North East Network, pp. 56-79.
10. *Ibid., op. cit.*, pp. 545-546, cit. Support Services to Counter Violence Against Women in Manipur: A Resource Directory, North East Network 2002, pp. 56-79.
11. *Ibid., op. cit.*, 546 cit. Menon Sen, Kalyani and A.K. Shiva Kumar (2001), Women in India How Free? How Equal?, pp. 56-78.
12. L. Keivom, Tipaimukh, Past Present and Future, pp. 11-12 cit. in Editor Lal Dena: *Dialogue on Tipaimukh Dam*.
13. Field Study.
14. *Ibid.*
15. *Ibid.*
16. *Ibid.*
17. *Ibid.*
18. Frank van Lierde, Author, We Widows of the Gun.

19. Field Study.
20. *The Sangai Express*, 11th September 2012.
21. Venetia Salem *op. cit.* p. 40. Deepti Priya Mehrotra, Burning Bright, Irom Sharmila, p. 81.
22. Swati Thakur, *op. cit.*, pp. 507-508.
23. Year wise Statement of Crime Against Women from the Year 2006 to 2011 (till September) for the State of Manipur.
24. Field Study.
25. Ranjan Yumnam, Best Time to be a Woman cit. in the *Sangai Express*, 18th Nov. 2012.
26. Ch. Priyoranjan, Border Trade in Manipur, pp. 202, 213.
27. *Ibid., op. cit.*, p. 214.
28. 9 Checkings between Moreh and Imphal, *The Sangai Express*, 4th July 2013.
29. *Ibid.*
30. Veneti Salam *op. cit.* p. 39 cit. H. Sudhir, Conflict, Vulnerabilities, Human Rights, Peace: Building and Polciy Agenda in the Contemporary North East, p. 500 cit. in Editor, Anisur Rahman, *Human Rights and Social Security*.
31. Venetia Salam *op. cit.* p. 38 cit. Tingneichong Gangte, Women's Role in 20th Century Manipur: A Historical Study, *op. cit.*, p. 141.
32. Chinnoy Kanti Biswas, Insurgency and the Tribes of North East India p. 93 cit. in Editors Ranju R. Dhamala and Sukalpa Bhattacharjee, *Human Rights and Insurgency, The North East India*, 2002, Shipra Publications, Delhi.
33. Sukalpa A Bhattacharjee, State, Insurgency and (Wo) man's Right, Two Cases from North East India, p. 132, *op. cit.*
34. Field Study.
35. R.S. Jassal, Militancy and Conflict Resolution in Manipur, p. 7.
36. Prasenjit Biswas, Nations from Below and Rebel Consciousness, p. 144 in Editors, Ranju R. Dhamala and Sukalpa Bhattacharhee, *op. cit.*
37. Ventia Salam *op. cit.* p. 38 cit. Goutam Biswas, Rights Consciousness and the other, p. 181. *op. cit.*
38. Gaikhamsin Riamei, Violation of Human Rights in North East India, pp. 37-38.
39. Ventia Salam *op. cit.* p. 39 cit. A. Pinto, H. Jubita, Community Response to Violence Against Women in Manipur, p. 8.
40. Esther Chinnu, Violence Against Women in Manipur, p. 50 cit. in Editors H. Sudhir, Jubita Hajarinmayum, *Violence Against Women in North East India*.
41. Lokayan Bulletin, Voices from India, July-October 1995, p. 106.
42. Heisnam Kanhailal, Manipur Society and Its Art and Culture cit. in *The Sangai Express*, 5th July 2013.

43. Ventia Salam *op. cit.* p. 39 cit. A. Pinto, N. Pamei, L.M. Lohriu, Violence Against Women in Contemporary Indigenous Societies, Structural and Dynamic Triggers, Attitudes, Remedies and Solutions, p. 5.
44. Field Study.
45. Deepti Priya Mehrotra, *op. cit.*, p. 85, pp. 185-186.
46. Salam Irene, Women Today with Special Reference to Manipur cit. Mahbub-ul-Huq Development Centre 2001, Women in South Asia.
47. *The Sangai Express*, 10th July 2013, Public Consultation on Tipaimukh, Dam.
48. C. Mathew Kamei, Tipaimukh Dam and the Zeliangrong Nagas, p. 170 cit. in Editor Lal Dena, *op. cit.*
49. David K. Zote, The Issue of Displacement and Rehabilitation, pp. 241-242, *op. cit.*
50. Ginneiching Simte, Towards the Protection of Indigenous Land Rights, p. 215, *op. cit.*
51. L. Hingneilam, Dialogue on Tipaimukh Dam, p. 226, *op. cit.*
52. Ventia Salam *op. cit.* p. 10 cit. Swati Thakur, Insurgency Aftermath Devstation for Women p. 506 in Madhy Rajput, Editor, *Social and Cultural Stratification in North East India.*
53. *Ibid., op. cit.*, p. 507.
54. N. Jayshree Devi, History of Women's Education in Manipur upto 1947, p. 43 cit. Saroj Nalini Arambam Paratt (Translated) The Court Chronicle of the Kings of Manipur: The Cheitharol Kumpapa, 2005 p. 47, and W. Lukhoi, Lai Haraoba. Manipur State Kala Akademi, Manipur, 1989, p. 21.
55. Field Study.
56. Salam Irene, Alcohol and Drug Related Violence Against Women in Manipur, p. 63 cit. in. Editors H. Sudhir, Jubita Hajarimayum, *op. cit.*
57. Ahanthem Anita Devi, 2012. Repetition of Manipur Women's Tattered Existence, cit. in *The Sangai Express*, 24th Jan. 2012.
58. Sanatombi Angomcha, The Hypocrisy of Patriarchy cit. in *The Sangai Express*, 7th July 2013.
59. N. Jayshree Devi, *op. cit.*, p. 85. cit. R.K. Sanahal Singh (compiled) Yakairol, August 1931, Manipur State Kala Academy, Imphal, 1991, p. 25.
60. *Ibid, op. cit.*, pp. 85-86, cit. Randhoni Devi, Meitei Niya Mangley Lairik Heirabadi Mangloidara in R.K. Sanahal, *op. cit.*
61. *Ibid*, cit. Kh. Nimaicharan Singh, Manipur da Prithivigi Ani Suba Lanjao Amasung Eina Angang Oiringei, R.K. Singh Khuraijam, Imphal, 1997, pp. 60-62.
62. N. Jayshree Devi, *op. cit.*, p. 86.

63. N. Vijaylakshmi Brara, A Situational Analysis of Women and Girls in Manipur, p. 116.
64. *Ibid.*, The Seen and the Unseen, p. 84 cit. in Editors, H. Sudhir, Jubita Hajarimayum, *op. cit.*
65. Samarjit Kambam, Model Women of Manipur, cit. in. *The Sangai Express*, 10th July 2013.
66. Field Study.
67. *The Sangai Express*, 15th July 2013.
68. *Ibid.*
69. *Ibid.*, 17th July 2013.

4

Violence against Women

Is Endemic and Escalating

Violence against women is endemic, it is institutionalized and it is continuously escalating. The one single factor which is the main cause for Violence Against Women is the fact that Manipur is suffering from a conflict situation. The seeds of discontent were sown as early as 1949 (The Merger Agreement) but the conflict became manifest in the public domain largely from the 1980's onwards.

The North Eastern part of India has remained disturbed since Independence. Some experts categorize it as 'one of South Asia's most disturbed regions). Violence, bloodshed, armed conflict are easily associated with this region, as this ethnically and culturally rich area has been engulfed by the fire of insurgency shortly after independence. Insurgency is a political movement which arises because of the unrest and dissatisfaction prevailing among the masses. It has also been termed as 'low intensity conflict' which has wreaked havoc for the people in the North East. While insurgency has affected life in general, it has had devastating effects on women of this region. As Heidelberg put it, "it is estimated that close to current war casualities are civilians, the majority of those are women and children, compared to a century ago, when 90 per cent of those who lost their lives were military personnel.[1]

Why Women? According to a World Health Organisation July, 1997 report "Women may be idealized as the bearers of a cultural identity and their bodies perceived as 'territory' to be conquered. Troops may also use rape and other forms of violence against women to increase their subjugation and humiliation'[2]. Manipur is now the most violent theatre of conflict in the North East region of India. In a memorandum submitted by a civil society coalition on Human Rights in Manipur to the United Nations in 2012, Violence especially VAW can be attributed primarily to: Manipur suffers from a breakdown of good governance, and a preponderance of military civil action programmes in lieu of state responsibility to development and welfare commitments. Institutions of the state have failed to respond to people's needs in total disregard to their rights and entitlements. Corruption is rampant in official circles; there is a general lack of commitment by the local political leadership to public welfare and respect for the rule of the law by all entities has alarmingly diminished.[2]

Half a century of imposition of Armed Forces Special Powers Act of 1958 (AFSPA) has on the one hand escalated discontentment and on the other institutionalized impunity and militarism in Manipur, The AFSPA grants extraordinary powers to the armed forces of the Union. In areas declared to be 'disturbed' even a non-commissioned officer of the armed forces has powers to fire upon or otherwise use force, even leading to death, of any person who is acting in contravention of any law, or is in possession of deadly weapons, or against an assembly of five or more persons arrest without warrant and with the use of necessary force, anyone who has committed certain offence(s) or is suspected of having committed offence(s), enter and search any premise(s) in order to make such arrests. No legal action can be taken up against the armed forces unless prior sanction is obtained from the Union Government.

The act created a culture of impunity and in extreme cases, gave carte blanche to commit rape, torture and carry out custodial killings. Opposition to the AFSPA resonated widely in Manipuri Society and is epitomized by the continuing over 12 years fast undertaken by a young Manipuri Women Irom Sharmila, who has vowed to continue her action until the Act is repealed[3] Why did Sharmila commence this fast the most unique Non-violent protest and the longest in the annals of Manipur's history? In reaction to an unprovoked killing of ten innocent people waiting at a bus-stop at Malom near Imphal airport by the Assam Rifles in November, 2000.

Ms. Rashida Manjoo, United Nations Special Rapporteur on Violence Against Women at a press conference in Delhi following her visit to Manipur in April 2013 remarked; Many women in the North East region are subjected to continued abuse, ill treatment and acts of physical and sexual violence. Chronic under-development in the region, coupled with frequent economic blockades, is having an impact and is exacerbating the already vulnerable situation of women and children living in the region. In conflict areas, such as the North Eastern States, the law protects the armed forces from effective prosecution in non-military courts for human rights violations committed against civilian women among others, and it allows for the over-riding of due process of human rights protection. In the testimonies received, it was clear that the interpretation and implementation of such an act (AFSPA), is eroding fundamental rights and freedom—including freedom of movement, association and peaceful assembly, safety and security, dignity and bodily integrity rights for women in Jammu and Kashmir and in the North Eastern states. With special reference to Manipur she cited that the lack of response from the police is the norm, with the attitude being that 'missing girls' are considered as eloped. 'I am deeply concerned about other consequences of such disappearances of young women including exposure to sexual abuse, exploitation or trafficking.'[4]

Women are the easiest targets for violence, sexual abuse and harassment—the very sight of a male in uniform is traumatizing[5] Despite the existence of women associations which are strong and powerful bodies, women are in the periphery in the decision making process but in the front line in any physical movement.[6] As a result, the conflict has perpetuated a cycle of direct violence, this climate of violence extended in the public sphere resonates in the private sphere too, where because of high tension, stress, fear and insecurity, domestic violence not only occurs, but is increasing both in intensity and frequency. The AFSPA is a trigger for the violence that engulfs women.[7] In contrast, some in the state are of the opinion that despite the continuance of AFSPA, army atrocities have registered a steep decline, (linked probably to Manorama's death in 2004 followed by the Nude Protest of Twelve Women before the Gates of Kangla) and it is the police especially the commandos who are responsible for VAW. The state police are for the most part comprised of local people and they are confident that they will not be called to book. Moreover, women are afraid not just physically of the police, but of their power which intimidates them to an extent where they are afraid to file a complaint or even an FIR. And the power of police permeates the private space-many personnel indulge in out of marriage dalliances/ affairs especially with young women- even those still in school. Their wives and children are afraid in general to protest, least the repercussions be even more dangerous-but they bear a burden of humiliation and shame, especially as Manipur is a small state where the cover is blown in an instant.[8] Some in the force themselves believe that excesses are committed which lead to a trust deficit on the part of the public in the police. But no crimes are committed by police under AFSPA as the act is not applicable to them. In fact it is the army that very often does not hand over arrested persons to the nearest police station within twenty-four hours; they prefer to interrogate the arrested in their own camps.[9] This may be partly or entirely true, but it does not detract from the fact that women believed that police commandos are always ready to unleash violence—women are caught in the crossfire for e.g. The pregnant woman who was killed in such cross-fire in 2009—Rabina Devi. In this context, in a report EN Rammohan IPS (Retd), former advisor to the Governor of Manipur stated; "In Manipur, civil policemen and officers were selected and trained as commandos. Although they did a good job initially, they soon deteriorated into a state terrorist force due to faulty leadership. They started extorting money from the business community.[10] Since then their reach has considerably widened. However when the force was set up in 1979, Former Inspector General of Police, ThanjamKaruna Maya Singh told Tehelka—'They were told to fire only when fired upon and pay special attention to the needs of women, children, and the elderly'[11]. And then there are excesses committed by the Indian Reserve Battalions in Manipur. 'In the wee hours of March 22nd last year (2012), two IRB personnel along with two others gang raped aUmorok (Chilli) seller at gunpoint in Bishnupur district. (She has since received justice although more than a year later) What makes the crime even more appalling is that a police sub-inspector provided a pistol which was used by the assailants to intimidate the victim while they were pillaging her modesty. In the last few days, news is a flush, about four IRB personnel deployed at Khuga Dam having captured a love-making scene of two consulting adults in the thicket, on a mobile phone with the criminal intention of blackmailing the unsuspecting victims, the clips of which has now been circulated online. What ails the IRB?—the impunity that accompanies the mindset of these criminals in uniform suggests the absence of a prescribed code of conduct. The unsaid fear among officers to even reprimand delinquents in the force is well known. Even the State Government seems reluctant to weed out renegades, the State DGP down to the Inspector has failed to curb mercenary adventurism of their boys. What is stark is the congruence of the societal decay in vogue with the degeneration in the IRB, and by extension, the state police. The root cause is the criminalization of the administrative system of Manipur, the police being only a small part, Manipur's society glorifies 'wrong doing'; the public will not so much as bat an eyelid to pester and offer bribes to anyone to have their way, right or wrong[12].

The state of Manipur is the most serious victim of conflict violence in North East India. As women are viewed as soft targets, they are inevitable engulfed by the fire of violence. According to the report of the Government of Manipur 2006, between 1999 and 2005, the number of crimes against women was, 2006—102 cases of rape, 39 cases of kidnapping and 174 cases of molestation. In 2008, 150 cases including 16 rape and 17 murder cases among others were recorded in the state. This was higher to about 99 cases of 2007 and 105 of 2006[13]. But the year wise statement of Crime Against Women as recorded by the police from the year 2006 to 2011 is as follows:

Table 4.1: Year-wise Statement of Crime Against Women from the Year 2006 to 2011 (Till September) for the State of Manipur.

Sl. No	*Head of Crime*	*2006*	*2007*	*2008*	*2009*	*2010*	*2011 (Till 31/12/ 2011)*
1.	Murder	7		10	14	12	2
2.	A/ Murder					4	6
3.	Culpable Homicide					1	
4.	Rape (Custodial)						
5.	Rape (Other)	23	20	35	31	32	31
6.	Kidnapping (Female)	68	83	70	97	107	89
7.	Dowry Death						
8.	Molestation	24	70	36	39	27	23
9.	Assault	49		33	10	15	17
10.	Cheating					1	1
11.	Criminal Breach of Trust						2
12.	Cruelty by Husband & Relatives		15	26	25	18	35
13.	Sexual Harassment		1	1	2		
14.	Other IPC not included above	36		14	2	6	9
	Total =	207	189	225	220	223	207

Table 4.2: Local Acts and Special Laws

1.	Immoral Traffic (P) Act		1	1			
2.	Suicide					10	4
3.	Child Marriage Restraint Act	–	–	–	–	–	
4.	Dowry Prohibition Act	–	–	–	–	–	
5.	Prevention of Food Adulteration Act	–	–	–	–	–	
	Total =		1	1		10	4
	Grand Total =	**207**	**190**	**226**	**220**	**233**	**211**

Source: Venetia Salam *op. cit.* p. 42.

Violence is perpetuated by both the security forces as by non-state actors. The editorial in a local daily stated that the centre in continuously assisting the North Eastern states by deploying Central Armed Police forces to assist the state police in their counterinsurgency operations against militant outfits and augmenting and upgrading the State Police force by way of sanctioning Indian Reserve Battalion. At a rough estimate, the strength of central security forces, including the Army, the Assam Rifles, CRPF and BSF deployed in Manipur must be around 50,000—an appreciable strength in a state with a population of around 27 Lakh and a geographical size of 22,327 sq. km. Bombarding the place with thousands of troops and armed not only with the latest sophisticated weapons, but also with an Act (AFSPA) under which anyone can be suspect and be killed but without declaring that a warlike situations is in place-war in a state of undeclared war.[14]

What is the impact of such a large number of forces on the population in general and women in particular? It has been stated that the army in its operations aims at fighting and neutralizing 'militancy' and not 'militants'. The malaise has to be fought, the insurgents are only a manifestation. The army never refers to the insurgents as 'enemy'.[15] This statement may be correct to some extent because the army atrocities which include murder, rape, torture, destruction and displacement are not mere punitive retaliations, but are meant to be a display of might and power of the state. It is aimed at terrorising the entire community, traumatizing and outraging them to such an extent that the community is emotionally paralyzed, physically inebilitated, and intellectually demoralized for any revolutionary ideology to ever appeal to them again; they become subservient to the state ruling over them. This is illustrated by a horrifying incident that took place at Oinam on July 9, 1987. Two pregnant women were forced to deliver their babies in full view of the jawans. Prior to this, on March 4th, 1977, a young girl was raped in Nagaprum Village of Ukhrul District by officers of the 95 Border Security Forces. The girl who was raped in front of the villagers, subsequently committed suicide.[16]

A young innocent woman, Luingamla, a chubby faced teenager was shot dead by Mandhir Singh, a captain of the Madras Regiment. She was alone at home in her village in North-East

Ukhrul district of Manipur. Captain Singh and a lieutenant entered the girl's home and raped her. When she resisted, Captain Singh shot her dead. In commemoration of Luingamla's strong spirit, her neighbor Zamthingla Ruivah wove a special fabric—a red kashan, signifying Luingamla'sinnocent blood, which was shed for the cause of women's dignity and honour. It is now worn as a sign of protest and solidarity.[17]

On 11th March, 1996, provoked by the attack of NSCN, the 20th Assam Rifles used women as human shields, by placing the muzzle of their guns on the women's shoulders. One Ms. Kanchungla was made to cover Captain Sharma with a Naga Shawl while the army was approaching Huishu Village[18].

A much greater impact of the conflict on women was when life in Manipur came to a grinding halt after the recovery of the body of Manorama Devi by the police on July 11, 2004 in Bamon Kampu of Imphal. Just for being a suspect (not proved) of having membership in the People's Liberation Army (PLA), Thangjam Manorama was raped and murdered by the personnel of 17th Assam Rifles. But as per the arrest memo, nothing about her membership to PLA could be substantially proved. The jawans wrote an artificial FIR in which they had shown that they had recovered a grenade from the residential house of Manorama Devi. Moreover, they pumped ten bullets in the body of Manorama Devi to wipe out the evidence of rape.

This incident added flame to the fire in Manipur. On 15th July, 2004, while many sit-in-protests were going on at various parts of Manipur, 12 women belonging to various social organizations protested naked in front of the 17th Assam Rifles at the Kangla Gate. It was a shocking experience for everyone, when a group of conservative Vaishnavite Meitei women came out to the streets and stripped of clothes in broad daylight to shout at security personnel. Incidents of arbitrary detention, torture and even rape by security personnel becomes the order of the day in the state. This protest by women has exposed a hidden part of the repression in Manipur—the use of rape as a repressive weapon by the Indian Security forces. The womenfolk raised a numbers of slogans, questioning how long they have to suffer, while their sons and daughters are being trampled on, tortured, raped and killed by the security personnel.[19]

Rabina Devi and her unborn child died as collateral damage, a death by structured insanity. The day the tragedy happened she was with her two and a half year old son. Not only was he witness to his mother's death, but left alone in shock; some kind-hearted passer-by kept him and later gave him to the police. Rabina's family only got to know of the tragedy while watching the local television network (Similarly in the book—'we widows of the Gun', one of the women learns of the death of her husband in a fake encounter from the television news). Where does it go from here—the violence? Is it so ingrained in the political culture that there can be no break from it? As Prof. LokendroArambam put it; "The tension of our lives is such that violence, viciousness and corruption in the environment, are undermining moral imperatives[20].

In countering the hegemony of power of the Indian State Insurgency does not succeed in overcoming the logic of power. It is a game of power which in its patriarchal essence is neither philosophically liberating nor is politically revolutionary. It is violence or power thrust for the hegemony of either the State or Insurgency, because both have statist agenda in which the woman is conspicuously absent. The ethnic woman of the North East suffers the imposition of ethnic males makes regarding preservation of traditional customs and costumes during ethnic movements, mostly without a decision of their own[21].

Marginalisation, indifference, resentment and hatred, are the acute causes of the violation of human rights in the politically out stationed North East region of India. Both insurgency and counter-insurgency in North East India have some justificatory logic from their respective stands points which cannot get together, as they do not have a sharable world view and telos. Even to imagine a relational trust, and consequently a confirmation of otherness on the part of any of these two parties inclined to reject the other, or to usurp the lead in the battlefield is a well-nigh impossibility. Rights consciousness, be it with the insurgents or the counter-insurgents has a clear collective connotation in this case, and it is ostensibly divorced from the notion of the other[22].

Army interrogation is anything but a dialogue (the same premise could be applied to non state actors). It bears the typical power to annihilate the other form the very beginning. It actually terrorizes the other to such an extent that he/she loses his/her being and becomes a ghostly shadow with fear and trembling, tottering on the brink of nothingness.[23] This is borne out by the stress/trauma experienced by most women when they are confronted by a man in uniform. During raid and searches, army jawans usually misbehave with the women. At the slightest pretext they lay hands on women, pull them by hand, pull away their clothes, sometimes actually strip them naked, (no reported incidence of this in Manipur), molestation and attempted molestation are occurring every day. Operations of insurgent outfits often exhibit the dominance of a collective ego, an absolutely community based approach to human reality, and thereby a de-recognition of others in and outside the community. This has sociological, political and economic reasons. Such reasons are vaguely conjectured and very often manifest (not systematically), when the insurgents of North East India conceptualize their relation with the state or the mainstream politics as an unequal one, or as that between the 'coloniser' and the 'colonized'. Operations of counter-insurgent forces do not exhibit the slightest proximity or affinity with human nature. In their methods of interrogation and torture, and by their whims during mass raids, human rights are violated straight away. Far from speaking of human nature, they deny the minimum existential and subject status to the human body.[24] In a list of Extrajudicial Execution committed by State and Central security forces in Manipur since January 1979 till May 2012, 17 are women including Manorama Devi and Rabina Devi and a young woman Farida of fifteen years. Of these seventeen killings, three were by the Manipur police inclusive of commandos, eight by the Assam Rifles and four by CRPF (Central Reserve Police Force), one by the army and one incident in which the Assam Rifles was involved was a combined force of both the army and Assam Rifles[25].

Strafing of civilian areas and the 'grouping of villages', turned army operations into full fledged war, making more distinctions between combatants and non-combatants, though now the overall situation has improved. Military still has an upper hand, while harassments at checkpoints and aggressiveness during search and cordon operations are stoically accepted as part of normal life in the North East, people express their resentment and agitate for their rights when a major incident involving large scale destruction of life and property of the civilian population, results from indiscriminate unprofessional attitude of administration. The impact of conflict on women is:

(i) widows of the insurgents are forced to earn for their livelihood and survival of their children (this is equally applicable to Widows of the Gun).
(ii) Increasing responsibility within and outside the household has resulted into declining health of women (exacerbated by rising costs for health care as also little or no time to access health care).
(iii) Fear psychosis and sleepless nights are common to Manipuri women,
(iv) Torture and rape of women by armed forces is an ugly truth[26].

Women are indeed caught in the cross-fire between state and non-state actors. The National Commission of Women has reported that 25 women and girls, most of them minors, were raped, molested and assaulted by militants in Tipaimukh sub-division of Manipur. It was reported that 18 armed militants raped 15 girls aged between 15 and 27 years, on the night of January 16, at Lungthulien, forcing the villages to flee to neighbouring Mizoram the next morning.

A study conducted by the commission observed that "The region, under the shadow of conflict, has witnessed a resurgence of patriarchal values and norms which bought with them new restrictions on the movement of women, the dress they wear and more overtly physical violence such as rape, which is systematically used as a tactic against a particular community. All this is compounded by the long social, economic and psychological trauma of armed conflict'[27].

Another incident of VAW inflicted by non state actors was not physical assault of women, but rather rendering her bereft of both husband and a daughter—double edged violence. In July 2013, the KLO/KLA Home Secretary, SeikhohaoKhongsai while travelling in a car with his wife and children was gunned down, his two and a half year old daughter Hoijoukim was hit by a bullet and succumbed to her injuries. The slain Secretary left behind three other daughters (14th July, 2013)[28]. It is not possible to understand the trauma of the inconsolable widow Nenei who in one instant, was deprived of both a husband and child. Can she overcome the horror of a senseless killing, and go on with her life—where will her support come from? These are questions that demand on answer, because this is not solitary incident; conflict has increased the number of single women headed households.

A major form of VAW is depriving her of a husband, son, even a father. In what circumstances can the taking of human life be justified? There is no war in Manipur, but; 'Manipur is today on the map of terrorism and we can no longer pretend otherwise by cloaking acts of terror with some more 'acceptable' form of violence such as insurgency or militancy or extremism'. Apart from the blatant acts of terrorism such as targeting the public by exploding bombs in public places, bombs are now placed near the gate or courtyard of residential homes and as it is women who raise early in the morning to clean the courtyard before performing their religious devotions; they are consequently vulnerable to violence if the bomb remains un-detected and is detonated, terrorism can also come under different modes, such as firing at the house of a government official or a businessman for monetary demands. Abducting and kidnapping for ransom, and at times finishing off the captive even when the ransom demand has been met, will certainly come under acts of terrorism. Violence sponsored by state is another instance of terrorism. It is time to come to terms with this harsh reality, for the fact stands that today, people no longer feel as safe as earlier about venturing out for the days marketing or shopping.[29] How many innocent women have lost their husbands or male relatives in such acts of terrorism? How do they go about reconstructing their lives? May be widows from the affluent sections of society do not have to struggle to provide for their children or for their own livelihood. But in common with all other widows, the emotional scars remain embedded and the trauma continues—how does one cope with the loss of a husband to a bullet or a bomb? Widows who even when their husband were alive struggled to make a livelihood are now rendered destitute with no viable means of livelihood. And they are mentally and emotionally shattered by the loss of their dear ones. 'Neither the state nor the insurgents have showed much sensitivity to the sufferings of ordinary people'. Undergrounds groups resort to violence against the state and nurture feuds amongst themselves, with innocent citizens ending up as the worst sufferers. The state is wreaking violence not only on insurgents, but also on non-combatant citizens, whom it claims to protect[30].

As Irom Sharmila herself a victim of violence (being nose-feed forcibly and detained in the security ward of government hospital ever since she commenced her indefinite fast in 2000) points out: 'strong army presence in Manipur has intensified the trauma of common people. Ordinary citizens are trapped in a no win situation—a cycle of deprivation and violence with no end or revolution in sight. The rights of ordinary people are being violated daily. The counter-insurgency policy in Manipur is one of suppression rather than negotiation. Genuine public grievances are not addressed, there is overwhelming reliance on repressive legal and military measures. Corrupt and manipulative governance is a major factor contributing to escalation of insurgent violence'. E.N. Rammohan, ex-superintendent of Police in the north-east acknowledges that in Manipur, armed forces have committed excesses on innocents. He writes that transparency and accountability are essential, if counter-insurgency is to be effective[31].

Irom Sharmila the Iron Lady of Manipur is an example of VAW. What can justify locking up a woman undertaking a peaceful protest in a security wing of a hospital at Imphal, administered by the Sajiwa Central Jail. She a young woman, then in her twenties, has been confined to a solitary existence for over twelve years. Women are generally referred to as both emotional and talkative—yet we have an example of a valiant young woman living a life alone, with no support system in place. Her only support is her faith in herself- that what she is doing is right—AFSPA must be repealed. And she has the courage to continue—despite the trauma she is continuously undergoing—a saga of annual arrests and confinement. The Swiss journal 'Le Courier" carried an article by Marc Oliviera Parlatano in April 2007, noting that Irom Sharmila's is the longest political fast ever recorded. Calling her a 'living icon of liberty famished Indians' he mused; 'It is utopic in the present militancy and political environment, but at least, in war-town Manipur, a handful of citizens do not capitulate in front of guns'[32].

Two cases cited in the book 'Burning Bright" highlights VAW 'contemporary writing in Manipur is replete with images of people suffering human rights violations. Leibakalai, a poor hardworking woman returns home one evening to find both daughter and son killed by security forces in a combing operation. She becomes mentally deranged and takes to wandering the streets, picking a fight with any security man she sees. In another village, Lairek, an elderly women, is arrested and imprisoned simply because she took in a young boy who knocked at her door one night, wiping his wounds, and feeding him scraps of food.[33] A humanitarian act of a woman being misunderstood and derided.

In this context a retired army colonel writes: 'Militarisation of societies is worrisome not so much because of the threat to life (particularly women and children) and property, but because of its flagrant violation of normal human inclinations to ask for their rightful place in society, and freedom to live and let live. This applies to both state actors as well as the commoners. Initially well intentioned to accord 'complete' freedom from a perceived 'enemy' the non state actors have forced the state actors to become offensive. More often the general public has to prove its innocence; and unless and until so established beyond doubt, people are rounded up in markets just to minimize deterrence on public'[34]. Such instances of rounding up create a major fear psychosis in women—they live in trepidation that at any moment, their husband or son will be arrested or interrogated, tortured and even killed. As a result women develop high levels of anxiety and depression.

Women affected in the conflict develop social/sexual difficulties and fears of stigmatization in their own families and in the wider society. Women are often compelled to sell liquor, drugs and sex for their own family's basic survival needs.[35] Every year more young women are exposed to the illegal commercial sex market. The number of commercial sex workers in Manipur stood at 9000 in 2006.[36]

A report of the Zee Research Group, ranks Manipur as the second most trigger happy state, just behind Uttar Pradesh. Manipur has 62 cases of fake encounters but none of these has received the importance given to the Ishrat Jahan case in Gujarat. In the report of the Supreme Court probing six fake encounters in Manipur filed by EEVFAM (Extra Judicial Execution Victim Families Association, Manipur) and Human Rights Alert, the Supreme Court has come close to 'rapping the State Government on its knuckles for giving a free rein to the police, especially the police commandos'. The State Police do not come under the provisions of AFSPA, but the fact that they are all involved in fake encounters as exemplified by the conclusions of the Hedge Committee, says something significant about a design at work. Catch them, whisk them away, and eliminate them and place gun on the dead body and come out with an encounter story. Such a story could not have been chartered out and implement without the knowledge of the political masters. It is this sense of immunity and impunity granted by the political establishment that the thuggish side of the police personnel regularly comes out in full public display. Cops on their fancy motor bikes, whizzing past the one way traffic. Honking away at the vehicle ahead with lathis waving, and at times using their lung power to throw invectives to give them the right of way, are spectacles, which Imphalites have witnessed regularly[37]. The army, paramilitary forces also do not posses any road etiquette and cause hazards to women's safety, especially in the crowded market streets. And the four IRB personnel, who were remanded to judicial custody in connection with video taping a young couple in the nude and uploading it on the internet, were granted bail in just about ten days. Low conviction rate has often been cited by prominent jurists in the country for the rising crimes graph against women. The Churachandpur episode (just referred to) should be seen beyond four rogue men in uniform—about the rot and gradual decay of the institution of agencies which are there to police the people[38]. The large numbers of security forces in Manipur pose more of a threat to women in contraindication of their mandate to protect women. And there is a greater threat when feuds occur between different security forces as for instance the July 16th 2013 incident when an Assam Rifles team stormed the Jiribam Police Station and assaulted the police personnel. A public protest with women in the forefront was launched against this incident—because in any conflict greater collateral damage is inflicted on women.

Conflict related violence constitutes a major share of the news every day, women appear to be the main targets of violence, as incidents of rape are reported almost on a daily basis. Except in the case of the perpetuators of rape against a U-Morok woman trader, most perpetuators get off scot free. This increase in violence as reported in the media especially in the last few years is in stark contrast to the years 1997 and 1998 where the percentage of cases of VAW was only 2 per cent and 6.5 per cent respectively[39]. Rape by civilians which was a rare phenomena is now a common phenomena despite the rapist knowing that the local community will not only ostracize him but also burn down his house. VAW with the state or its agents as perpetuator is a fact of life in the North East region for several decades. The enduring climate of this violence with impunity, committed as it is, by state agencies has a peculiar impact on the image of violence in society and the image of the state. The state instead of being perceived as the protector of civil rights and an upholder of law is perceived as the chief violator. The political nature of the violence, its use as a weapon of intimidation and terror by the state is well understood by the community, certainly by the community of women[40].

The reality and threat of such violence looms over women's everyday lives, colouring their ability to participate and engage fully in society and to exercise democracy. The experience and fear of violence is a constant threat in women's lives, intertwined with their most basic security needs. It limits women's choice directly by destroying their health, disrupting their lives, and constricting the scope of their activity; and indirectly by eroding their self-confidence and self esteem. It is also believed that women who experience rape are of bad or questionable character. Rape is also linked to concepts of chastity, morality and family honour. So much so, that often for a victim, registering a case, can be an added traumatic experience. Hence when rape occurs it leaves the victim vulnerable to shame and social stigma. It is also true that women in a vulnerable situation (as in conflict ridden Manipur) are exposed to the dangers of rape.[41] That is why a call was made on MeiraPaibi Martyr's Memorial Day, 12th April 2012 to intensify the MeiraPaibi Movement as the rate of crimes against women have been escalating. In fact many women's organisation have been demanding the death penalty for rapists, including 'hanging to death in public places'. Rally protests by women against violence are often forcibly disbanded the application of force usually results in minor or grievous injury to some of the protestors. Recent years have witnessed atrocities meted out against women in most visible ways. And in each and every incident the violence is stark, brutal and inhumane. The case of Premila (who was raped, killed, and her body burnt by petrol ignited over it) is a stark reminder of the prevailing state affairs. This incident occured in April 2012.

'It renders earlier understanding of our (Manipuri) society as gender sensitive and a society where women are accorded a high status as compared to other societies as misplaced. On the one hand, VAW has come out from the invisible condition, tradition covered by layers of patriarchal and social mores to the visible domain. This is true as far as domestic violence is concerned. On the other hand the alarming trend is the increase in violence committed against women in the public domain by strangers e.g. The gang rape and killing of ThangjamManorama, rape and killing of a woman at Pheiyeng, gang rape of a woman at Bishnupur and others. It indicates that the culture of violence and militaristic method of settling issues in the society has spilled ever from the military to the civilian population. This is on account of the prolonged and continued violence in the state which influences the everyday life of common men and women'[42].

However the Social Welfare Minister A.K. Mirabai introduced a novel scheme christened "Financial Assistance and Support Services to Victims of Rape" with a view to ameliorate trauma and social stigma generally endured by victims. Manipur is the first state in the North East to launch the scheme. To implement the new scheme effectively, Criminal Injuries Relief and Rehabilitation Boards have been constituted both at the state and district levels.[43] The Minister rightly deserves accolades, but at the same time except for a single instance of some rape victims getting financial assistance, nothing is known of the working of the Boards at a time when rape is almost a daily occurrence, except for Churachandpur District Social Welfare Officer N. Umarani who distributed cheques of ₹ 40,000 each to two rape victims of the district. There are instances reported of abduction of women by unidentified gunmen and the culprits not being brought to book. At a consultative meeting on atrocities on women and children an advocate opined that legal justice against the criminals who committed crime cannot be delivered because the police do not conduct the necessary investigation—so crime against women increases[44].

In the prolonged armed conflict, women and children have been especially vulnerable to state repression. Besides, exposing them to the ravages of internal armed conflict, they have been subjected to physical and mental torture, degrading treatment, sexual abuse, arbitrary detention, harassment and extra-judicial killings. It has become a common practice amongst the security forces including the police, engaging in counter-insurgency operations, to do away with the safeguards accorded to a women by the criminal procedure code, while dealing with 'suspects'. Arrest by male security personnel, interrogation in army camps and police stations, torture and sexual abuse (including rape) by male security personnel in custody has become routine. Two sisters in Imphal East were picked up by Central Reserve Police Force (CRPF) on 14th January, 1999 on charges of sheltering underground activists. The all male team of CRPF took them to their camp at Pangei, stripped them naked, beat them with iron rods and sticks. Despite filing for redress, justice has been denied. Out of dozens of rape cases by security personnel only in one, were the rapists tried and punished. Most rape by the army goes unreported due to fear of social stigma, and the futility of taking up a embarrassing legal battle against the might of the army. A girl's modesty comes under suspicion, once she is arrested by the police or security forces, and detained in their custody[45]. All too often, women are left to defend their rights—this increases their vulnerability to violence. For instance: suspected militants attacked a Patrol of the 15th Regiment near Tabanglong village bus station, killing one army personnel and injuring four. Just then, a bus plying on the road came to the place. The Army asked all the passengers to come down from the bus and assaulted all the male passengers and detained them. The army forced the same bus to carry the dead body of the army personnel and the four injured to the battalion headquarters of 15th Jat Regiment stationed at Tamenglong. While doing this, the army used women and children passengers as human shields, by forcing them to sit in the bus along with them.[46]

Another uncalled for instance of VAW occurred on 5th October, 2004, Laishram Mira was brutally beaten up with firewood by a Manipur police commando at KhumanLampak Bus Terminus. The police commando team reportedly vent their ire on the old woman after they failed to arrest gamblers in the area.[47]

As part of 'Operation New Kangleipak' armed cadres of the KYKL (a non-state actor organization) abducted eight teachers, including two lady teachers. While the males were shot in the leg, the women were caned for allowing malpractices in the ongoing National Institute of Open Schools, Manipur, examinations[48]. Violence has become the way of self-determination because the presence of the Indian state in the North East is absolutely contradictory to the development of indigenous energies[49]. Since VAW is commonly associated with the promulgation of AFSPA, the Justice Jeevan Reddy Committee in its report to the Home Ministry on 6th June, 2005, suggested that AFSPA be repealed 'AFSPA has become a symbol of oppression, an object of hate and an instrument of discrimination and high-handedness'. In this context, the Former Governor of Meghalaya R.S. Mooshahary stated in November 2009, with reference to removal of AFSPA from the North East in general and Manipur in particular; If the Act is removed, I think the situation would not worsen. In fact it will improve. The Act has made the people vulnerable'[50].

And with the reference to 'encounter killings' in Manipur which have devastating effect on women, whose status changes from a wife to a widow, the Supreme Court stated; 'If one innocent person is killed by police or other security forces in a fake encounter, it creates tremendous upsurge of hatred. People know whether an innocent person was killed by mistake or deliberately. The Asian Human Rights Commission commenting on the report of the Commission of Inquiry constituted by the Supreme Court says that in all cases of extra judicial executions in Manipur, the security forces have blatantly violated the law and procedure and have engaged in cold-blooded murder, that the use of disproportionate force against the victims by firing at them repeatedly at close range is standard practice, the complete negation of all legal procedures even by administrating officers including executive magistrates, open and uncontrolled possibility for wanton use of authority, including fabrication of, or destruction, or tampering of the evidence and the crime scene, and the abysmal failure of the draconian law, the AFSPA, coupled with the perpetual imposition of emergency under Section 144 of the Criminal Procedure Code 1973 has resulted in administrative failure, and extra-judicial execution is definitely not the way to deal with anti-state activities in the state. The Commission referred to a witness statement given on oath by an Army Major 'I did not know the identity of the deceased—I came to know the name after the same was published in the newspaper. The Commission said that in all cases involving extrajudicial execution, the pattern is that after killing a suspect, the authorities charge the person of an offence under the Unlawful Activities (Prevention) Act.[51] Amnesty International India said that an independent panel set up by the Supreme Court to investigate 6 alleged extrajudicial executions in Manipur has found damning evidence of impunity and abuse of special powers by security forces, resulting in widespread human rights violations. The continuous use of AFSPA for decades in Manipur has evidently had little or no effect on the situation. On the other hand, the six cases which have been shown to be not real encounters are egregious examples of the AFSPA's gross abuse.[52] A woman activist from the hills was of the opinion that fake encounters have reduced in the hill areas in contrast to the valley. But women's organizations formed to protect men are vulnerable to violence by both police commandoes and the IRB. This is why tribal hill women do not want the IRB to be stationed in any hill district—they violate laws and create and perpetuate conditions of fear and insecurity. This fear she stated even affects the animals (domestic) kept by women in their homesteads or paddy fields. Fear is all pervasive-women are not safe and their future is uncertain. The elected representatives of the people, Ministers and MLA's are not the true representatives of the people because they have bought the votes of the populace and in administration are guided by own self interests. They do not bestir themselves to create conditions of normalcy.[53] The impunity granted under AFSPA continues to violate the rights of women—by depriving them of both a husband and breadwinner, and also by inflicting others forms of violence on women themselves (e.g. The use of women as human shields). Widows are forced to earn through whatever means are available, legal or illegal, for their own and their children's livelihood. Some of the options for livelihood pursued by them, strip them of all semblance of dignity—for example; sex work, selling liquor/drugs- and such options are not made from free choice, but from necessity.

But the senseless killing of Manorama Devi in July, 2004 drew the attention of national and international scholars to the trauma of the Manipuris. But followed as this infamous incident was by the Nude Protest by twelve women, AFSPA was lifted from Greater Imphal on 12th August, 2004—a victory for women. Corruption is a major impediment in the path to justice, exacerbated by lack of legal knowledge, despite efforts directed towards the same. The women of Manipur have been impacted by the armed conflict, irrespective of circumstances.[54] They become victims of the situation either as relatives of armed activists, relatives of state officials or as shelter providers.[55] On the one hand there is the constant fear of being hounded by the state armed forces for being sympathizers, and on the other, they dare not refuse the armed combatants. Even if there is no overt threat by the militants, there is the increased economic burden and the constant concern for the safety of the family.[56] This is intensified because of the government policy of militarizing and weaponizing Manipur; exacerbated by the proliferation of non-state actors groups, all of whom control human life through the use of threat of guns. Non-violent solutions to put an end to conflict are not properly explored, despite SOO's (Suspension of Operations) signed between the government of India, the Government of Manipur and some non-state actor groups. Moreover civil society continues to remain fragmented inclusive of women's groups. No neutral international organization like the United Nations is permitted to intervene, and so women's plight is not addressed either by state or humanitarian agencies in a manner as to prevent VAW[57].

All families experience the trauma of conflict, rich, poor, men, women, but the impact differs especially for those who are forced to provide protection to non-state actors in their homes. So also women who lose husbands to the conflict suffer much greater trauma. But a nation state has the right to use force, even kill, for legitimate reasons. As such a policeman when he beats a person is only doing his duty. But when a state starts to kill its own people, there arises the necessity of controlling the state. If a non-state actor inflicts violence, the victim can approach the state for redress, e.g. women whose husbands have been killed. The problem is that when it is the state that allows violence, no remedy/redress is available especially to widows. Moreover women are often viewed as shelter providers or informers to parties engaged in conflict. As a result VAW is inevitable.[58] Moreover as the police are the enforcers of the law, the law cannot generally be used against them. The police as a force display an appalling lack of gender sensitivity. Regarding the charge that the police do not investigate crimes properly and prepare charge sheets, the police are hampered by inadequate forensic laboratories, and by the fact that before they arrive at the crime scene, it has already been disturbed.

There is a close link between VAW resulting from conflict and domestic violence. Since the entire population lives in an environment of fear, insecurity and uncertainty, people live literally on the edge; as a result even small domestic issues which in a normal environment could be quickly and amicably resolved, are apt to ignite and burst into a conflagration. When disagreements arise between wives and husbands, the latter are quick to resort to physical violence, to release their own pent-up tensions and fears. Sometimes this physical violence only escalates as time goes on and both wife and husband remain obdurate. Men who have been harassed or tortured by parties engaged in conflict, tend to be more short-tempered—so also men who are engaged in conflict. Because of the intimate relation between wife and husband, most cases of domestic violence are not reported. For instance, a disturbed, fearful husband wants some private space for himself so he locks his wife out of the bedroom, compelling her to spend an uncomfortable night on a mat unrolled on the floor or on a sofa, where she tosses and turns till dawn, when she gets up unrefreshed and extremely anxious—unable to second guess her husband's behaviour in the morning. Then there are other husbands, especially elderly husbands who rise when it is still dark, because they cannot sleep through the night and wake up their wives to attend to their needs, in most cases the wives are working women who require their sleep, especially in light of the fact that most women are the last to go to bed at night because of their multifarious duties and responsibilities. And there is no equitable distribution of household chores- it is taken for granted that this is women's work.

Because society does not remain static but continues to evolve, the traditional joint family system of Manipur based on mutual co-operation and co-dependence, where the bonds of family ties were extremely strong has given way to the emergence of nuclear families. The usual practice in a nuclear family is that both parents work primarily to ensure a better life not only for themselves but their children. However the 'better life' envisaged is calculated in material terms—the acquisition of more wealth, moveable and immoveable assets. This in turn enables parents to raise their standard of living and also provide a better more expensive education to their children both within and outside the country. In fact, few well-earning parents would refuse their children's request to study in countries outside India where the cost of living, also that of education, is many more times that of India and especially Manipur. The necessity to earn more and get more, places great stress on both parents—they spend most of their time and energy in their workplace and return home tired and weary. They develop a tendency to snap at each other for trivial reasons when they return home. Continuous bickering often ends in domestic violence which generally feeds on itself becoming a continuous circle of violence. Both wife and husband are deprived of the support, guidance, counsel and advice of elders especially parents and grandparents, whose presence in their house would have mitigated the causes for domestic violence to a considerable extent, if not eliminating it altogether. Also the high moral values and ethics of the older generation are not used to defuse domestic violence in nuclear households.—Nuclear parents themselves have little time, energy or inclination to fulfil spiritual/religious duties on a daily basis and they justify their actions on their heavy workload. They thus deprive themselves of that inner spiritual strength which would prevent incidents of domestic violence. And few such parents seek advice of elders or spiritual guides.

Earnings of nuclear households are adversely impacted by continuous inflation and endemic economic blockades and recurrent bandhs. This creates more stress and tension in the family because their financial liquidity is threatened. And stress translates into vulnerability to violence on the domestic front. Quarrels between children and parents is also on the rise—if a mother takes the side of her child, the husband is angry and takes out his ire on her.

Another cause for domestic violence is when women earn much more than their husbands. Such women usually highly educated spend their earnings as they desire—this often causes resentment silent or vocal in the husband, leading in course of time to aggressive behaviour. This is especially so in cases where husbands are unemployed or do not work—they become frustrated and frustration vent itself usually in mental and emotional violence, creating an atmosphere so brittle and uncertain that women are adversely impacted.

The lowering of ethical standards is also responsible for domestic violence. Many married men indulge in post—marital affairs, especially men in position of power. Manipur being a small state with a small population, news of extra-marital affairs spreads fast and results in humiliation to the wife combined with loss of respect and even a lowering of her status especially in social gatherings. Infidelity in marriage has been exacerbated by the use of mobile phones and the internet which permit married man to make clandestine assignments. Of course, there are times when the communication is completely above board, but it still arouses suspicion, mistrust and fear, the wife is afraid that at any moment her husband may take a second wife. The reverse is also true- young women especially those lacking a sense of morals as also responsibility, sometimes walk out of a marriage, without even trying to make the marriage work-giving feeble excuses, that the husband is an addict or possesses some undesirable habits or character. But cheating on one's partner is more from the male side. The adverse consequence of extensive use of the mobile for no apparent reason sometimes has fatal results. A man with a wife and three children became habituated to chatting, albeit innocently with a woman over the phone—a woman whom he had not met or seen. However the woman in question believed that the man cared for her and so without informing him she searched out his house, and came to his home to meet him in person. Not only was the man taken aback, but his wife was flabbergasted when she learnt that the woman had come to ask her husband to marry her. The incident immediately resulted in not just violence to the intruder but her death, so as to eliminate the threat to the couple's marriage[58]. In several instances, a husband will accuse a wife rightly or wrongly of infidelity, to provide him with a reason to inflict violence on her. But it is not just men who are perpetuators of domestic violence. There are many mother-in-laws, who in their youth or middle age have experienced violence. They in turn inflict violence on their daughter-in-laws directly or indirectly—some even try to retain their hold over their married sons and use all kinds of ruses to keep the husband and wife apart. Moreover, the victim has no support system to fall back on. And even if she did it is hampered by the fact that each individual is so busy that they don't have time or the energy to come to the victim's rescue at the moment when she is in dire need of help—especially moral support. When they do find time the victim has already faced trauma and depression alone while the support system was engaged in working to improve the quality of their own lives.

Also, society especially Meitei society being conservative, parents tell their daughters that they must continue to endure, because they are now members of another family—the family they are married into. And in general Meitei parents do not visit their married daughter on a regular basis—only on social occasions primarily associated with the passage of rites like the birth of a grandchild, marriage or death of a family member. Some parents to save their daughter from violence send them to study and work outside the state, and to carve out a career elsewhere. But young women from Manipur studying or working outside of the North-

East region are even more vulnerable to violence—sexual assault and molestation.

There are also good mother-in-laws who unwillingly, with no malice, inflict especially mental stress on their daughter-in-laws. Many such women suffer from Alzheimer's and as a result keep asking the daughter-in-laws repeatedly to perform the same task or because of mood swings, they suddenly take umbrage-accusing the daughter-in-law of stealing their son, or stealing money or jewellery or ransom household articles. Sometimes they lock themselves up in a room creating heightened tension, because a woman suffering from dementia can set a house on fire, by leaving a gas cooker unattended or a kerosene lamp (which could spill and ignite). Sometimes such women rush outside without proper attire or footwear, heedless of traffic on the road. This exposure to danger causes great trauma to the daughter-in-law who is responsible for caring for her. Dementia also causes some of these women to constantly berate their daughter-in-laws; there is no support service for the daughter-in-law who is the main care-giver. Others abuse the maids working in the house—the maids leave, increasing the work load of the daughter-in-law who usually is a working woman.

Another raison d'être for domestic violence is the prevailing culture of consumerism. The traditional awonpot/gifts to the bride by her family has been replaced by expensive consumer items which burns holes in the pocket, gives rise to stress because expenditure on such items often involves taking loans at exorbitant rates of interest, which is difficult to repay when the payment is due. Debts and mortgages are thus a trigger for VAW. Parents compete to provide substantial, costly dowries. Brides who bring to their married home a small or insufficient dowry are often subjected to violence not only by the grooms, but by their in-laws. The constant taunts and harassment, verbal and physical, drives many young wives to commit suicide by ingesting some chemical or pesticide.

Grown up children also inflict violence on their mothers. In their desire to be independent they cut off the ties that bind mother and children in a loving relationship. They also tend to communicate less and less with their mothers. So a mother in her autumn years is left to fend for herself—deprived all too often of not only the presence but also the affection of her adult children. The adult children will no doubt visit their mother when she is critically ill or in hospital and in case of death, will pay minute attention to performing the last rites. What these adult children fail to realize is that what mothers want is for them to keep the channel of communication always open, to come to them for love and support when they are alive, healthy and well and to give them opportunities to care for and interact with their grandchildren. Unfortunately, both women and adult children rarely make use of counselling or support services to mend broken relationships—in the twilight years, the mother as also the father are left alone, deprived of affectionate companionship of children and sometimes also grandchildren. This is the worst kind of violence that a woman has to endure. Even in the age of technology—adult children do not have the time or inclination to either phone or E-mail their parents.

Since all household works are the so called 'exclusive domain' of the woman, woman especially working woman have the right to demand that their unpaid work at home be appreciated not necessarily by accolades, but by the absence of complaints from family members, especially husbands. Yet the latter continually complain—the food is not to their liking—it is too salty, too bland, too greasy or it is not ready on time, or it is not served as a hot meal. This last is especially relevant to evenings and late nights when husbands socialize outside the home with their male friends, return home and expect their wives to be waiting for them to serve their hot meal. What about the tired working woman—especially the women vendors in the marketplace—who serves them even a cup of hot tea when they return home exhausted from the day's labour. And the stress is greater for women whose husbands return home drunk (Manipur is officially a dry state, yet liquor is available just about everywhere but not in legalized liquor outlets) these men are apt to quarrel and inflict violence, verbal or physical on their wives. Wives are defaulted and abused on other counts as well—the house is not properly cleaned/maintained, the clothes are not properly washed and ironed, the shoes are not shined and so on. No cognizance is taken of the fact that the males of a household are quite capable at least physically of performing these tasks. Yet they are content to smoke, sip tea and gossip, while their wives trudge long distances to carry water on their heads and firewood on their backs.

For the ordinary working woman whose economic role is viewed as marginal and supplemental, and who enjoys no benefits like maternity leave, provident fund, pension, health care benefits, etc. her confidence is continuously eroded—she is unable to make decisions on her own, even if she were permitted to do so. This loss of confidence makes her a suitable target for domestic violence. Women who are financially insecure are equally vulnerable. Since the family is a private sphere, violence in the family is not addressed by law or the police.

When the state remains mute and passive, and given the prevailing environment of violence, domestic violence also escalates. Working women especially those who have shattered the glass ceiling, resent being treated as typical housewives, forced to multi-task, in order to maintain the sanctity of the patriarchal ideology.

Some forms of discrimination against women stem from tradition and custom which can lead to domestic violence; a century ago the literacy rate of women in Manipur was low (in 1951, there were only 6,962 female literates), but in 2011 it stands at 72.4[59]. It stands to reason that discrimination practiced against illiterate women, will not be submitted to by educated women, especially those in the highest echelons of society or in the top ranks of their profession, if men attempt to do so, inevitably domestic violence results. Amongst the Meitei Pangals, misusing of talaq is a common practice, and divorced women are usually deprived of alimony and also deprived of the 'mehr' (bride price) promised in the nikah nama[60].

Domestic violence is neglected in Manipur-one of the most obvious reasons for this is the magnitude of state violence, and violence in tribal conflicts, beside which the magnitude and the frequency of domestic violence appear trivial. In Manipur, domestic violence is inter-linked to overall societal stress due to the high levels of violence and it legitimization. The pressures of economic, cultural and political deprivation of rights, impact deeply on the close knit families and clans. Alcohol and other chemical abuse in the communities have reaped a rich harvest of domestic chaos and uncertainties, leading to violence[61].

Domestic violence is also a result of alcohol and drug dependence. The average age at which Indian men develop alcohol dependence is 29 years. Despite prohibition being in force in Manipur for more than two decades, and illegal drug use being recognized as a public health emergency (in 1995) alcohol and drug use is common among all sections and strata of society. Use of liquor is also customarily related with traditional rituals and festivities, especially in the hill areas of the state. Practically in every village, liquor is brewed according to the requirements of the people-rice beer and liquor. Women are especially vulnerable to alcohol and drug related violence. This is a definite link between increase in alcohol intake and increase in wife and child abuse. Any individual under the influence of alcohol, loses his inhibitions and in any inebriated state doesn't think twice about inflicting insults humiliations on his wife, even though when he returns home she would be fighting to stay awake. Drunken men are also apt to pick quarrels with wives at the drop of a hat. Many wives prefer not to answer any query of a drunken husband, but the latter will goad the wife to retaliate—the end result being violence—verbal, physical, emotional, mental. The woman is shamed when the returning husband is unable to walk straight or falls down ignomously, either in the sumang, house or even on the road. Moreover the women witness trauma because of reckless driving of drunken spouses. It also diminishes a woman's confidence and self-respect.

Drug users on the other hand are violent in a more subtle manner i.e. in manipulating a woman into unsafe sex, unsafe injecting behaviour, and unplanned parenthood. The women became vulnerable to communicable diseases like STD's and HIV, and to unsafe abortions in the event of the user or the woman herself not wanting a child. Most women bear alcohol or drug related violence silently for fear of stigma and discrimination.

The international centre for research on women estimates that

60 per cent of women face violence at some point in their marriage, because women are vulnerable to abuse in intimate relationships. They tend to wrap their identity around their marriage which reportedly provides her and the children with security. Women being givers, focus so much attention on their husbands and children, that they have no private space for themselves. They are also so wrapped up in the new identity revolving around marriage, that they fail to provide themselves with a safety net, when the marriage runs into difficulties. Where violence is seen as a means of monitoring and correcting women's behavior, women maybe as likely as men, to believe that it is appropriate to beat a woman for certain transgressions, including covert contraceptive use, Many young women (especially those who elope) have inadequate knowledge of reproductive health's and rights and are easily manipulated through control over their sexuality and fertility. Young men too are often as ignorant of women's physiology and anatomy, but unplanned pregnancies and parenthood impacts a woman very differently. It is she who will be responsible for caring for the child, whereas she maybe too immature to undertake the responsibility.[62]

A recent fear that has surfaced is the use of the 'rape drug,' to make women complaint to sexual advances. Rape drugs have been in existence in other places and countries for a long time—but its use, not yet properly documented, points to recent usage. It is also not known what drug is used, but incidents of lacing drinks with such a drug or suffocating a woman with a cloth immersed in the drug (to render her unconscious or comatose) have surfaced in the media. However adequate cognizance of women's vulnerability through the ministration of the drug has not been given the attention it requires. Also the use of, for instance pepper sprays to prevent a sexual assault is not practiced in Manipur, because such preventive items are not sold in the state.

One section of women who experience violence are domestic maids, the majority of maids receive a meagre salary, are made to work from dawn to dusk and into the night hours. They are deprived of leisure time and even a day off in the week, they are not provided with benefits associated with salaried working women. Because of the pittance they receive as wages, they are unable to leave the job and return home, especially maids who come from rural areas or from neighbouring states. They are vulnerable to harassment and exploitation and their insecurity is exploited.

Women especially young women are constantly subjected to eve teasing, molestation, assault, these is an ongoing debate that it is the woman who invites assault generally because of the manner in which she is attired. There is no doubt that every individual has the right to dress as per their choice, but simultaneously appropriate dresses are to be worn on particular occasions such as weddings, etc. as also in the public domain, and especially when travelling in public transport. The new wave of globalization and consumerism as also modernism has radically changed the style of clothing. Simultaneously climatic changes especially global warming necessitates the use of lesser, more comfortable clothing. So young women wearing short skirts or shorts are not using inappropriate attire, however there is a time and place for the use of such clothing, and scanty, revealing dresses worn in public do attract unwarranted attention and make the wearer vulnerable to violence. They need to remember that the law is not a neutral force in patriarchal societies, and cultural and religious norms and values reinforce and justify existing power structure.[63]

It is a well known fact that wherever there is inequality, more poverty in households and wherever there is growing unemployment then the main burden of it is borne by women. A woman today has no guaranteed work, accepts instead any kind of work for a salary for below the minimum wages and in some cases on worse terms. When economic vulnerability increases, the degree of abuse, sexual or on women's dignity, leads to an increase in VAW. They are not given their due recognition for their worth which exacerbates VAW. The women bear the brunt of all misfortune and hardship and most men believe that women should be housebound,[64] even if they earn outside the home-the responsibility of the home devolves on them. Because of the intensity and continued occurrence of domestic violence, especially physical abuse, a section of such women are reporting this violence to the Department of Social Welfare, Government of Manipur, and a minimum of ten cases are reported daily. But an impediment encountered by the majority of such women is that they are either ignorant of the provisions of the Domestic Violence Act 2005, or are unable to understand its provisions. Moreover, the lawyers engaged by them are not primarily motivated to secure justice for the women-they are concerned with their own remuneration, and neglect giving proper advice to clients. They instead negotiate a quick settlement, whereas in most cases the violated women are entitled to a larger settlement. They often do not fight for the woman to retain custody of the children maybe because of traditional tribal customary practices in this regard. However these practices are not applicable to Meitei and Meitei Pangal women. Sometimes, a woman has to buy back her child from a husband who has left her and remarried. The following tables indicate the number of cases in court with reference to Protection of Women from Domestic Violence. In the table surprisingly the total number of cases is extremely small as also the number of pending cases registered between 2005 to 2010. Similarly in 2011, there were only 18 applications and appeals filed[65]. In contrast, a government source revealed that perhaps the low number crimes reported is because domestic violence occurs mainly in families where the man or head of the family is himself a government officer. Many of them maltreat their legal wife and have a part-time live in relationship with other women, some of these women are also provided a home to stay in, there normally is no divorce nor any kind of legal recognition to such live-in-relationships, perhaps because they are not permanent. With reference to domestic violence, it normally takes the form of wife beating, and a survey revealed that much of this beating is instigated by the mother-in-law. So it is a double form of VAW.

However, no Naga women have complained to the authorities dealing with domestic violence-the complainants are usually Meeteis followed by Meitei Pangals. In crimes committed under the Domestic Violence Act, women usually suffer from deprivation of property or residential rights. Cases of incest as also unnatural sex have also been reported as also domestic violence of senior women citizens. In some instances, the mother-in-law, to retain her ties as also authority over a grown-up son, creates conditions in the home where wife and husband have to sleep in separate bedrooms. Early marriages also make women vulnerable to domestic violence including unsafe abortions and unplanned parenthood. Young women who are drop outs from school or college are more susceptible, and as they lack both skills and knowledge, they become progressively submissive, and lose the right to make decisions. The climate of violence in the state inevitably resonates in the private sphere and triggers a cycle of continuous violence. Failure of the judicial system to provide relief/justice to women adversely impacts them. And husbands who are harassed or tortured by security forces or non-state actors, tend to take out their frustration on their wives. In cases of inter-community or interfaith marriages, the new daughter-in-law is often discriminated against through subtle actions, resulting in destroying her confidence. At the other end of the spectrum are the well educated professional women whose achievements give rise to tension in families, where the male head is earning little or nothing.[66]

Domestic violence because of the intimate relation between husband and wife is generally not reported, and as counselling has not yet become popular in Manipur, and because of paucity of qualified counsellors, women continue to be subjected to such violence. If a woman marries a man who professes a religion other than her own, she is usually counselled to convert to the husband's religion-this is an infringement on the rights of women. And even when she is allowed to practice her own religion, she is usually made to carry out religious rituals related to her husband's religion, whether she desires to do so or not. What the husband conveniently trends to forget is the fact, especially when it is a love or non-arranged marriage, is that when he proposed to the lady who would subsequently become his wife, he proposed knowing about her nature, beliefs, religion, etc. and accepted her as she was. But once married, the perspective of the man changes, he expects the wife to fall in line with his own likes, dislikes, traditions and customs. Marriage is a give and take. This principle applies equally to husband and wife. Our women have been the victims of the impact of various causes of violence viz. poverty, divorce, judicial separation, conflict status quo, alcoholism, drug abuse, economic disparity, unequal power equations etc. Yet the strong sense of subsistence and survival compels them to be the source of sustenance for their families.[67]

Another easily avoidable cause for domestic violence, is that in a conflict state where ethnic feuds and tensions continue to dominate popular consciousness, in cases of mixed marriage, inter-tribal, inter-community, the daughter-in-law is discriminated against subtly or overtly by family members. As narrow walls rise to contrict one's mind, thinking grows increasingly more insular. This gives rise to two kinds of families—(1) families under stress (2) broken families. When a husband and wife hold diametrically opposed perspectives, because of their different upbringing, background, religion, this phenomena occurs and impacts children-children usually do not lack material possessions, but are deprived of parental affection, support and care. But children, especially teenage children are also guilty of violence against their mothers. If a mother does not concede to their desire, whether for money, material goods, permission to stay out late, attend parties, drink, they create a climate of heightened tension within the family which literally pushes the mother against the wall. She is often forced to borrow in order to buy new clothes, new electronics, a bike or car for a son or daughter just to restore a semblance of normality and peace in the house. The mother herself will often be using public means of transport. She will continue to be violated by continuous demands, usually for money, from children, teenage and adult.

In order to ensure the visibility of women's presence in the public sphere, women's dignity and security which are largely violated in the private space of the family and personal relationship, are to be recognized and dealt with as human rights. Even violence meted out by mother-in-laws to daughter-in-laws must end. VAW is a critical tool in maintaining the relation of domination and subordination between men and women. It is all the more difficult to address because it is structurally integrated into most of the institutions of society. And while direct violence is visible and identifiable, the structural violence that women confront on a daily level is difficult to perceive.

And it is not only men but women too who perpetuate VAW[68] including female officers.

The question that arises is why victims of violence do not have recourse to law. It was reported recently that Manipur Police's lax approach in investigating criminal cases was recorded as the worst in the country in 2012, with the latest, National Crimes Records Bureau report, listing Manipur as having the Country's highest pendency rate (86%)[69]. And 'when law enforcers become law-breakers, innocent civilians become the first casualty.'[70]. This was clearly illustrated in the death of the innocent pregnant woman Rabina in 2009.

Often law is not faithful to the realities of life, it rather follows the logic of proofs. Many choose not to seek recource to law because of lack of awareness or resources. Law in the Indian context is unable to change the social reality-an intricate network of deeply ingrained beliefs and customs, manifest in various subtle and evident aspects of life. Unless accessibility to legal procedures and legal literacy is drastically improved, VAW would continue[71]. Moreover, lawyers are not perceived as women friendly-rather as individuals who want to earn the maximum they can from their clients. They fail to appraise women clients of all the dimensions of the case, and the relevant sections of law applicable to their case.

It does not mean that women are acquiescent to or passive about violence. We have several instances of women victims themselves coming forward in public to narrate the violence inflicted upon them-such acts reveal the inner strength and courage that women possess. And there are individual activists, female and male, and many, many women's organizations who take up cudgels on behalf of women victims. It is for precisely this reason that the u-morok trader (chilli trader) who was brutally gang raped in 2012, received justice in just one year-a feat that needs to be repeated for all such victims. On the other hand when police take cognizance of a rape committed, they tend to adopt a gender-insensitive stance in recording the victim's statement for instance in the case of the Yairipok rape victim (2013), perhaps because the alleged rapist himself worked in the police department.[72] And although the U-morok trader has received justice, the trauma of the ordeal impacts every minute of her life. According to the secretary of Women Action for Development Sobita Mangsatabam, over 300 cases of VAW including rape, murder, molestation, trafficking, brutal physical assault, abduction, intimidation, abandonment and intimation occurred in the state in 2012.[73] It is thus clearly apparent that VAW is pervasive, continuous phenomena, but if women victims continue to come forward in the public domain to register their complaints, a change must and will take place, albeit at a snail's pace. Women's movements will have a similar impact.

Table 4.1: No. of Cases in Court on Protection of Women from Domestic Violence Act, 2005 in Manipur as on 22/10/2010

Sl. No	*Period*	*No. of Cases Registered*	*No. of Cases Disposed*	*No. of Cases Pending*
		1. Name of District: Ukhrul		
1.	2007	Nil	Nil	Nil
2.	2008	Nil	Nil	Nil
3.	2009	1	1	Nil
4.	2010	2	2	Nil
		2. Name of District: Chandel		
1.	2007	Nil	Nil	Nil
2.	2008	Nil	Nil	Nil
3.	2009	1	1	Nil
4.	2010	1	1	Nil
		3. Name of District: Bishnupur		
1.	2007	Nil	Nil	Nil
2.	2008	Nil	Nil	Nil
3.	2009	7	7	Nil
4.	2010	12	Nil	12
		4. Name of District: Senapati		
1.	2007	Nil	Nil	Nil
2.	2008	1	1	Nil
3.	2009	Nil	Nil	Nil
4.	2010	Nil	Nil	Nil
		5. Name of District: Imphal West		
1.	2007	Nil	Nil	Nil
2.	2008	29	29	Nil
3.	2009	32	32	Nil
4.	2010	20	3	17

(*Contd.*)

Table 4.1: (*Contd.*)

Sl. No	*Period*	*No. of Cases Registered*	*No. of Cases Disposed*	*No. of Cases Pending*
	6. Name of District: Imphal East			
1.	2007	35	29	6
2.	2008	58	41	17
3.	2009	98	47	51
4.	2010	46	21	25
	7. Name of District: Thoubal			
1.	2007	Nil	Nil	Nil
2.	2008	22	22	Nil
3.	2009	6	6	Nil
4.	2010	5	5	Nil
	8. Name of District: Churachandpur			
1.	2007	Nil	Nil	Nil
2	2008	Nil	Nil	Nil
3	2009	Nil	Nil	Nil
4	2010	2	2	Nil
	9. Name of District: Tamenglong			
1.	2007	Nil	Nil	Nil
2.	2008	Nil	Nil	Nil
3.	2009	3	2	1
4.	2010	Nil	Nil	Nil

Table 4.2: Total No. of Cases Yearwise

Sl. No	*Period*	*No. of Cases Registered*	*No. of Cases Disposed*	*No. of Cases Pending*
1.	2007	35	29	6
2.	2008	110	93	17
3.	2009	148	96	52
4.	2010	88	34	34
	Total	381	252	109

No. of cases Disposed after Counselling: 680–381 = 299 nos.

No. 7/319/2007/SW
Government of Manipur
Department of Social Welfare

Imphal, the 7th July, 2012

To

The Commissioner (SW)
Government of Manipur.

Sub: Parliamentary assurance regarding details of cases received and disposed off since 2006—reg.

Sir,

In inviting a reference to Govt.'s letter No. 14/57/2010-S (SW) dated 3/7/2012 in concomitant to G.O.I letter No. 17-5/2006-WW dated 20/6/2012, on the above subject relating to Lok Sabha Unstarred Q No. 3152 dated 19/12/2008 regarding Pt-(d) of the question, I have the honour to furnish herewith the detail information as desired by the Ministry. Since the PWDV Act, 2005 was started implementing in our state from 2007, cases relating to this has been provided from 2007 onward.

Table 4.3

Sl No.	*Year*	*No. of cases filed under PWDV Act*	*No. of cases disposed off*
1.	2.	3.	4.
1.	2007	35	29
2.	2008	54	37
3.	2009	60	9
4.	2010	12	2

I am, therefore, to request kindly to forward the information to the Ministry for the parliamentary assurance for Lok Sabha Q No. 3152 dt. 19/12/2008 so as to fulfilled the assurance given at the earliest.

Yours faithfully,

(G. Satyabati Devi)
Director

Reference

1. Swati Thakur, Insurgency Aftermath Devastation for Women, p. 502 cit. *http:/manipuronline.com/features/armed conflict and small arms proliferation in India 2011/02/08 and* Heidelberg papers in South Asian and comparative politics http:/www.sai.uni-heidelberg.de/SAPOL, HPSACP.htm working paper no. 33, December 2007 in Madhu Rajput Editor, *op. cit.*
2. *Ibid., op. cit.*, p. 503 cit. World Health Organisation Report, July 1997.
3. Civil Society Coalition on Human Rights in Manipur to Christof Heyns, UN Special Rapporteur on extrajudicial, summary or arbitrary execution, March 2012, Mission to India.
4. *The Sangai Express*, May 3rd, 2013, Rashida Manjoo recalls 'visit' to Manipur, asserts AFSPA violates Intl Laws.
5. Venetia Salam *op. cit.*, p. 10 cit. Nandini Basistha, Women Managing Conflict: A Case Study of Manipur, p. 491 cit. Anuradha M. Chenoy, Militarism and Women in South Asia, p. 133 in Madhu Rajput Editor, *op. cit.*
6. *Ibid.*, pp. 497-498.
7. Field Study.
8. Field Study.
9. Field Study.
10. Civil Society Coalition on Human Rights in Manipur, Memorandum submitted to Christ of Heyns, UN Special Rapporteur on Extrajudicial, summary or arbitrary executions, March 2012, Mission to India, p. 8.
11. *Ibid., op. cit.*
12. Surendranath Laimayum (former 'Group A' CISF officer), What ails the IRB, *Sangai Express*, July 6th, 2013.
13. Anuj Kanchan Datta Roy, Human Rights, Women and Conflict

Situations: The Scenario in North East India, pp. 523-524, cit. in Madhu Rajput, editor, *op. cit.*

14. *The Sangai Express*, Editorial, 5th July 2013.
15. Venetia Salam *op. cit.*, p. 32 cit. Trigunesh Mukherjee, Insurgency in the North East: Improving Awareness pp. 58-59 cit. in Editors Ranju R. Dhamala/Sukalpa Bhattarcharjee, *Human Rights and Insurgency, The North East India*, 2002, Shipra Publications, Delhi.
16. *Ibid., op. cit.*, p. 63, pp. 75-76.
17. Sudeep Chakravarti, Highway 39, Journeys through a Fractured Land, 2012, pp. 72-74.
18. Venetia Salam, *op. cit.*, p. 31 cit. Swati Thakur, Insurgency Aftermath Devastation for women p. 504.
19. Nandini Basistha, pp. 496-497, *op. cit.*
20. Sudeep Chakravarti, *op. cit.*, pp. 134, 142, 147.
21. Sukalpa Bhattacharjee, State, Insurgency and 'Wo' man's Human Rights, Two Cases from North East India, p. 129 cit. in Editors Ranju R. Dhamala/Sukalpa Bhattacharjee, *op. cit.*
22. Venetia Salam, *op. cit.* p. 38 cit. Deepti Priya Mehrotra, Burning Bright, Irom Sharmila pp. 62-64.
23. *Ibid., op. cit.*, pp. 184-185.
24. *Ibid., op. cit.*, p. 187.
25. Civil Society Coalition on Human Rights in Manipur, *op. cit.*, pp. 27-104.
26. Anita Sonker and Shalini Gupta, Human Rights: Response and Challenges with Special Reference to North East, p. 266, p. 268 cit. in Editor, Madhu Rajput, *Understanding North East India*.
27. Swati Thakur, *op. cit.*, p. 506.
28. The Sangai Express, 15th July 2013.
29. *Ibid.*, Editorial October 2008 cit. in Deepti Priya Mehrotra, Burning Bright Irom Sharmila, p. 61.
30. Deepti Priya Mehrotra, *op. cit.*, p. 59.
31. *Ibid., op. cit.*, pp. 62-64.
32. *Ibid.*, p. 171.
33. *Ibid.*, pp. 158-159 cit. Yamini Devi, Combing Operation, pp. 121-126 and 'Dadi Ma Ki Peruk Kangsu', pp. 127-130.
34. Venetia Salam *op. cit.*, p. 10 cit. Sudeep Chakravarti–Highway 30, Journey througha Fractures Land 2012. p. 243.
35. H. Sudhir, Conflict, Vulnerabilities, Human Rights, Peace-Building and Policy Agenda in the Contemporary North East, p. 504 cit. in Editor Anisur Rahman, *Human Rights and Social Security*.
36. Bedavati Laishrm, An Account of Domestic Violence and Crime Against Women, p. 35. cit. in *The Orient Vision*.

37. *The Sangai Express*, Editorial, 18th July 2013.
38. *Ibid.*, 19th July 2013.
39. A. Pinto, H. Jubita, Community Response to Violence Against Women in Manipur, cit. Roy, L.D. Singh, S.D. (1999). Report of the Survey of Violence Reportage in the media of Manipur, 1997-1998.
40. *Ibid., op. cit.*
41. Angela Rangad (North East Network), *Violence Against Women in the State on the Rise*, 2002.
42. Yenning, An Agenda for Women Centric Movement in Manipur cited in *the Sanagai Express*, 20th May 2012.
43. *The Sangai Express*, 9th June 2012.
44. *Ibid.*, 21st June 2012.
45. Core, Women in Armed Conflict, *The Manipur Experience.*
46. Gaikhamsin Riamei, Violation of Human Rights in North East India p. 68.
47. *Ibid., op. cit.*, p. 243.
48. *Ibid., op. cit.*, p. 250.
49. Sudeep Chakravarti, *op. cit.*, p. 243.
50. *Ibid., op. cit.*, pp. 259-960.
51. *The Sangai Express*, July 20, 2013.
52. *The Sangai Express*, 25th July 2013.
53. Field Study.
54. Rajana Mishra, Gender Equality and Status of Manipur Women p. 554 cit. in Editor Madhu Rajput *op. cit.* cit. R. Goswami, Women and Armed Conflict, Ground Realities from North East, for Facilitating the Fulfillment of Government Obligation to Women's Equality, Women in Armed Conflict Situations, prepared by North East Network in collaboration with International Women's Rights Action Watch-Asia Pacific Kuala Lumpur, August 2005, p. 5.
55. *Ibid.*, cit. an article on Murder of Vasmi Khaleng decried in the *Sangai Express*, Imphal, September 14, 2011 p. 1.
56. *Ibid*, cit. Goswami, *op. cit.*, p. 19.
57. Field Study.
58. *Ibid.*
59. Y. Thamkishor Singh, Census of India 2011, Manipur Series 15, p. 34.
60. Salam Irene, The Muslims of Manipur, p. 76.
61. A. Pinto, H. Jubita, *op. cit.*, p. 5.
62. Salam Irene, Alcohol and Drug Related Violence Against Women pp. 64-66 cit. in Editor H. Sudhir, Jubita Hajrimayum *op. cit.*
63. Angela Rangad, *op. cit.*
64. Bedavati Laishram, An Account of Domestic Violence and Crime Against Manipuri Women, p. 35 cit. in *The Orient Vision.*

65. Refer to Table.
66. Field Study.
67. Bedavati Laishram *op. cit.*, p. 36
68. Rekha Roy, *op. cit.*, pp. 176-177.
69. *The Sangai Express*, 23rd June 2013.
70. *Ibid.*, July 6th, 2013.
71. Rekha Roy *op. cit.*, pp. 177-178.
72. *The Sangai Express*, July 2nd 2013.
73. *The Sangai Express*, April 7th 2013.

5

Conclusion

Women have always been held in respect and accorded honour in Manipur. But the Indian tradition is similar—however, cognizance must be taken of the fact that this respect is qualified in that it represents only one side of the coin. The Indian tradition envisages a woman occupying an important position in the household where she is loved and respected—but she remains in a state of constant tutelage—as a girl she is subject to the tutelage of her father, as a wife, to the tutelage of her husband, and as a widow, to the tutelage of her eldest son. This tradition has undergone some change over a period of centuries, and the last form of tutelage has disappeared to a great extent with the rise of nuclear households—the eldest sons as also other adult children are too busy pursuing both independent lives and careers. The Manipuri tradition is in its essential similar to the Indian tradition but right from the beginning of Manipur's recorded history, women as individuals and groups have exercised power and authority in different ways in different historical periods: the Meira Paibis are an example. But for every woman or group of women who have achieved success in academics, sports, dance, music, entrepreneurship, politics, civil services, health care, judiciary etc. there is a story of a struggle against innumerable odds to achieve the 'impossible'. Today, when the young women of Manipur are armed with the tools of a good education, even in a strife-torn society of endemic bandhs/ blockades/disruptions in daily life, women have reached the glass ceiling. Not only do these women deserve accolades but they must be viewed in the prism of models of success to be emulated and even surpassed by succeeding generations of women—as later generations will have access to new and more efficient forms and tools of technology in diverse fields—in the endeavour to achieve their goals they have before them examples of successful women in every generation and age.

The rise in salaried as also professional women, experts in the own fields/disciplines, raises the question whether the development, more concentrated in the urban rather than the rural areas of Manipur, will change the status of women to ensure that both at home and outside, they are genuinely empowered. At present this section of women are by and large still multi-taskers, and it is assumed that their professional work outside the home, does not mean that they are free of household chores and domestic responsibilities even if, and they usually do, have maids or other helpers to assist in routine household work. They still have to be the first to rise in the morning and the last to go to bed. If this situation continues to remain entrenched because of dominant patriarchal groups and traditions, then in practice women do not have the liberty to do as they please with their time, energy and earnings, and the tag of a high status accorded to women in Manipur rings hollow. And VAW both at home and outside is a fact of life which women have to live with. Recently an incident of an enraged husband chopping off three fingers of his wife was published in a local daily.

The President of All Manipur Women's Voluntary Association Kunjarani stated that 10 women were raped in Manipur till June 2013. During the period, two women were murdered after rape, 10 women died in a suspicious manner and ten others were murdered. The same period also witnessed abduction of five women and mysterious disappearance of eight women. Saying that these were only media reported cases, Kunjarani added that there must be many unreported cases as well (*The Sangai Express*, 27th Aug. 2013). The woman of the North East discovers for herself a tradition specific role that secures her a position of a subject within social bonding amidst the social distortions produced by the patriarchal dispositions of hegemony. An important section of women in the North East seem to have realized that: "Patriarchy which operates through gender caste, class and ethnicity" is integral to the problems facing women[1].

An indigenous writer wrote an article entitled 'Best time to be a woman'. He cited education—women are getting a decent education encouraged by their parents whose middle class aspirations extend both to their sons and daughters. Second—the change in the nature of economy: from manufacturing, agriculture and labour intensive industry to knowledge and service oriented economy has been a catalyst for women's empowerment. Women as a consequence may start earning more than men as they grab more high paying and prestigious jobs. A slew of new pro-women policies have been introduced into the workplace such as extended, meaningful childcare and maternity benefits. At home, as women hold bigger purse strings they have a greater say in family affairs. The effects of all these on men will range from feeling of resentment, fear to resignation, as also assault on a random woman on the street[2].

There is no doubt that women are forging ahead in education at all levels in the state from primary school to university, girls and women are topping the charts in different disciplines. And middle class women do want their daughters to benefit from a good education, within or outside the state or country. It is also true that many pro-women policies have been introduced in the workplace, but most of these are confined to the formal sector, and even there, crèches for infant children are not usually available to working mothers. Having a sizable or larger income does make a woman more confident, but that does not necessarily translate into greater decision making powers especially in the private domain, except in the case of a few families.

There is a new class of women entrepreneurs who have introduced pro-friendly work strategies for women employees. For example, one such young woman allows them sick leave, maternity leave—whether paid or unpaid is not as important as the fact that when a woman employer who has given birth to a child is ready to return to work, even after a year or more, her position in the company is assured. Also for employees who give up their jobs at the time of marriage—if the marriage runs into difficulties and the woman returns to her natal home, she can rejoin her work it is as though she never left. And women employers are more considerate of their staff—both women and men, they are given time off and also taken on outings such as a picnics, a shopping spree etc. or treated to a sumptuous meal. But many such women entrepreneurs face continuous stress associated with insecurity surrounding any business in Manipur as also vulnerability to extortion from different sections of the population especially non-Manipuris. So how can women be genuinely empowered? A mass sustained campaign on gender awareness and sensitization needs to be carried out, but the strategies are to be framed in the context of the culture, traditions and environment of Manipur. While preserving the former, the campaign should effect a radical change in the mindset of people—both female and male so that for instance, even traditional customary law, practiced in most areas of the state becomes gender—just and gender friendly. A married daughter must enjoy the freedom and right to return to her natal home in times of stress, crisis or difficulty, whether temporarily or permanently. She should not be viewed as a person who is living only temporarily in the family home i.e. until she is married off. And the tradition of parents maintaining a distance from the married daughters needs to be reviewed, because a daughter whether married or unmarried, remains a daughter to her parents throughout theirs and her lifetime.

The practice of gender budgeting also needs to be introduced both in the private and public sphere, and it needs to be incorporated as an essential principle by the government in its planning process. Knowledge of gender budgeting also needs to be widely disseminated and the Ministries of Social Justice and Empowerment and Women and Chi!d Development should take the initiative.

The right of women to landed property must also be clearly recognized and popularized, especially so, when in many instances it is the woman who have been responsible for the construction and maintenance of the family house. But for those are unable to build their own houses or buy their own farmland (Manipur having a predominant agrarian economy) provision must be made for all women, married and unmarried. They must also be provided with education in the field of technological advance, and frequent programmes for women on up-gradation of skills must be a component of the state's planning and administration, because financial security is an essential component in the empowerment of women. If a woman possesses no material assets, she is financially insecure, she becomes dependent on the male provider, and becomes submissive with no independent identity of her own. For this reason, although education has already revolutionised the life of women in the state, they need to be oriented with the new trends and disciplines in the sector of education, whether relating to environment, nano-technology, watershed management, scientific waste disposal etc. and girls on the threshold of becoming undergraduates/postgraduates must be counseled on the career opportunities existing in new disciplines and branches of education—this enables the young women to make an informed choice. Such strategies need to be designed that provide/create a positive bias in favour of women's empowerment. Although the Government of India had announced the National Policy for Empowerment of Women in April 2001, more than a decade later, many women in Manipur remain disempowered in ways that fundamentally impact their lives. Especially elderly women and widows who suffer from increasing neglect because of their infirmities that busy adult children have little time or energy to take cognizance of. On the contrary, since these women possess a special set of skills, honed over the decades, special arrangements must be made by governmental, non-governmental, community based organizations and the corporate sector to utilize these skills in a manner appropriate to the women concerned. For instance a retired women politician/activist could be engaged, part-time or full time, to teach her skills to the uninitiated. This would give elderly women some purpose or direction in life.

Adequate security must be made for marginalized women, those working in the informal sector such as maids and other women domestic helpers, unlicensed vendors, drug users, those infected with HIV, those divorced or separated. They should be provided with health care benefits, compulsory fixed days of leave in a year, counseling, low cost housing and sanitation, nutritious food at subsidized rates especially for those infected with HIV and other such benefits. They should be provided with vocational skills that guarantee sustained livelihood. Before such trainings are provided a market survey should be conducted to assess what goods or services are in demand.

Although the practice of chenba (elopement) is widely prevalent, pre-marital counseling including counseling on planned parenthood should be made mandatory for young couples entering into matrimony, especially those who are drop-outs from school or college and have no employable skills. This would ameliorate the difficulties young and immature women experience when they wed without understanding what constitutes the institution of marriage, and what rights and responsibilities go hand in hand with marriage. Life skill education is a must for all such women.

Women facing trauma as a result of all kinds of VAW must not merely be only monetarily compensated, but must be provided with swift and speedy justice, as also access to trauma counseling centres. Such centres staffed by professionals need to be set up in every district of the state, and women accessing counseling should not be discriminated against.

Women should neither be forced or voluntarily go in for abortion for reasons such as a child will interfere with their career, they are not ready to take on/responsibility of parenthood, they need to secure their position in the institution in which they serve etc. Despite strides in medical science which allow women even in their forties to conceive children, will they be in a position when in their sixties or seventies to give their children what they require other than material goods and assets? And will such older women be able to care for and nurture children/infants in middle age?

Moreover the new emerging middle class of self reliant, economically independent women tends to follow a life style which is subject to criticism in that it does not conform to traditional, societal mores. These women because they work hard, rightly believe that they have right to spend their leisure time in the manner they see fit. But a large number of such women are unable to achieve a balance, they party too hard and drink too much, their style of dress is not suited all too often to the public domain. There is also a perceptible decline in moral standards and values—an inclination towards the profane instead of sacred. Awareness on the sanctity of family life, marriage, ethical values must be conducted from the early years, so that these women do not neglect family, home and marriage, placing them on a back-burner, and do not indulge in pre-marital or extra marital relationships or resort to unnecessary abortions. Recently a letter published in a daily news paper decried the complete breakdown of public morality and ethics.

This could be related to the fact for ethnic women of North East, their culture and cultural rights are asserted in their celebration of self reflexivity in carrying out their gender specific roles. In a community which inscribes ethnicity on her sexuality and vice-versa, an assertion of Cultural Rights would mean 'becoming a woman' and as Elizabeth Grosz describes 'going beyond identity and subjectivity, fragmenting and freeing up lines of flight, liberating a thousand tiny sexes that identity subsumes under one. "In her predicament as ethno sexual subject she must celebrate a body without organs (Bwo) as Grosz states, which does not oppose or reject organs but—opposes the subordination of the body to exigencies of property and propriety"[3]. Since women as a whole whether empowered or not are multi taskers and inclined to neglect their personal health needs until illness overcomes them, subsidized health check-ups for women annually should be made mandatory, especially tests for breast/cervical cancer, T.B., hypertension, diabetes, etc. Those women who come from BPL families may be given subsidized nutritious, high protein food items.

Policies and programmes for women whether initiated by Government, NGO's, CBO's must necessarily incorporate women not only in the process of decision making but also implementation. Women know best what will benefit them in the circumstances and environment in which they live. And all such plans must be suitable to the way of living, customs and traditions of Manipur. There must be a mechanism to ensure that benefits actually percolate to the women for whom the scheme is devised. A scheme successfully implemented in Delhi may not achieve any success in Manipur even if properly implemented, because of the difference in standard of living and culture between the two places.

Since the inception of the planned programmes, the North East Region has been exposed to various development experiments. These programmes are developed without taking into consideration the socio-cultural context. As a result of the implementation of ill conceived planned programmes, and the sudden exposure of society to outside influences, certain disfunctionalities began to appear[4]. The object of sustainable development (specially for women) has failed to evolve. Incursions into the fragile ecology of the region led to the rapid depletion of resources, resulting in stiff resource competition among the various groups[5]. Inevitably the ethnic woman loses out.

Many of the benefits of government planning do not have the desired results. For instance—Primary Health Centres especially in the hills are dilapidated, bereft of necessary infrastructure, staff and medicines. The Sarya Shikshak Abhiyan provides for a midday meal, yet parents prefer to send their children either to private schools, or to work in the fields. The fact is that, the tribal economy in hill areas necessitates almost equal labour of all age and sex groups to sustain their livelihood. The grownup children remain engaged, in looking after the children and households, while their parents go for out-door work like jhumming, collection of firewood and forest products, etc. The general and well known factor hindering government's efforts for economic development of the hill people is the dishonest and unfair means practiced by a section of employees involved in the functioning machinery in distributing government benefits and implementing development measures at the grass root level (This pertains to the Imphal Valley as well). Need based measures need to be devised[6].

However from June 2013, many women of Churachandpur have actively engaged themselves in social policing especially in Bijang, formerly a rendezvous point for substance abusers, inclusive of both novices and girls. The women who begin policing from well before dawn into the wee hours of the night have substantially reduced the trafficking and consumption of drugs and alcohol. They substituted these with relief aid in the form of cash and foodgrains as also provided spiritual solace through prayer meets. Their efforts have been crowned with success and replicated in surrounding villages such as Tuibuong and Thinkangphai. The health of the former substance abusers has improved for the better, violence caused by intoxication has reduced, as former male drinkers, drug users now spend their time and energy more constructively, thereby improving the quality of family life.[7]

It must however be recognized that wine/liquor has been used in traditional, customary rituals of the tribals for centuries and many tribal women are engaged in brewing wine as a means of livelihood. They are often stigmatized and condemned for their choice of livelihood, but in the absence of alternate means of livelihood either by government, NGO's and church bodies, they are forced to continue to brew wine. These women needed to be provided with skill development which caters to consumers needs for goods, other than rice wine/rice beer. The efforts of these women which resembles that of the Nisha Bandhis in the 1970's needs to be applauded, because although prohibition has been in force in Manipur for more than two decades, liquor and psychotropic drugs are available all over the state.

Women's economic contribution is both recognized and applauded, but as most earners belong to the unorganized sector, their labour is not reflected in the GDP and so the paradox of Manipur having extremely high levels of poverty but no slum population is a unique feature of the state. As a result many women live on the level of subsistence, and despite long hours of work, are unable to improve their lifestyle because of an environment of continuous inflation, exacerbated by endemic bandhs and economic blockades. An example illustrates this truth: a single mother of four, quarries sand from the river bed from dawn to dusk, but her earnings enable her to provide only the basic necessities for herself and her children.

But there is in contrast the example of a young woman film-maker, whose work starkly contrasts with the video-clip that went viral on the Net of a nude couple—an act of so called moral policing by security personnel. A Manipuri documentary film "Gun and a God" is Sonia Nepram's directorial debut and has been selected for the prestigious Mumbai Women's International Film Festival. The film relates the journey of a woman who was victimized by the structural violence of society, a woman who found her voice in a gun and justice in God[8].

The lone woman Cabinet Minister A.K. Mirabai Devi ascribed the failure of Central Government schemes to uplift women, to women's continued dependence on men. Even elected women members seem to be influenced by their spouses, they need instead to exercise their constitutional rights. The government does distribute financial aid and instruments like sewing machines, but women must not only be financially independent, but must ably protect themselves against all forms of VAW[9]. An opinion expressed in a news daily asserts that tribal women who commute to Imphal daily to sell vegetables are short-changed because of lack of bargaining skills, lack of fluency in Meiteilon, time constraint, poor transport system[10]. There is a kernel of truth in this assertion, and their vulnerability needs to be addressed—however a Tribal Women's Market has been constructed in the capital city. However the tribal women need special measures to facilitate their economic functioning.

The fruit of knowledge is from our fathers and grandfathers, and the reserved wealth from our mothers and grandmothers". "Husband brings in firewood, wife brings all the other goodies". These old Manipuri sayings in the words of Yenning portray 'the basic concept of division of labour and interdependence between man and woman'. But the second saying prescribes only one duty for the man and many duties for the woman. 'Powerful female bonding practices coupled with the traditional institutions of female authority and autonomy have created a unique environment for collective political action'[11]. These statements are made in the context of asserting that despite interdependence between men and women, discrimination in any form was not practiced against women. But history, especially the historical truth that the Manipur Kingdom was constantly engaged in warfare especially against Burma and neighbouring hostile tribes and states, meant in practice, that women had to work all hours to support themselves and their family. The writer has attributed the concepts of democracy and development imparted from outside as a reason for erosion of the status of Meitei women.

However, there is no gainsaying the fact that if women are to be truly empowered, if they are to come into their own, they need to come together on one common platform, irrespective of ethnic and religious affiliations. At present the women's movement is fragmented, and the divide between the hill and the valley is stark. The women of Manipur have been through a baptism of fire to overcome all odds—there is no reason why unity between all women's groups cannot be forged. Because Manipuri women possess not only indomitable courage but an inner resilience.

References

1. Sukalpa Bhattacharjee, State, Insurgency and (Wo)man's Human Rights, Two Cases, from North East India, p. 129. cit. in Editors Ranju R. Dhamala, Sukalpa Bhattacharjee, *op. cit.*
2. Ranjan Yumnam, Best Time to be a Woman, *The Sangai Express*, 18th Nov. 2012.
3. Sukalpa Bhattacharjee, p. 132 *op. cit.* Elizabeth Grosz, A Thousand Tiny Sexes. Feminism and Rhizomatics in Topoi, Sept. 1993.
4. C.K. Biswas, Tanmoy Bhattacharjee in Introduction of Editors Ranju R. Dhamala and Sukalpa Bhattacharjee, *op. cit.*
5. *Ibid., op. cit.*

6. Chinmoy Kanti Biswas, Insurgency and the Hill Tribes of North East India, p. 96, *op. cit.*
7. *The Sangai Express*, September 9th, 2013.
8. *The Sangai Express*, 2013.
9. *The Sangai Express*, 2013.
10. *Ibid.*, Kamei Samson, Morality of Tribal Women's Livelihoods in Manipur, Oct. 30th 2013.
11. Yenning, Is the Meira Paibi Movement Facing Extinction, *The Sangai Express*, Sept. 15th 2013.

Index